What wives are saying about Susie Davis and *Uncovered* . . .

"Wow. *Uncovered* is just that—honest, open, gut-level talk about putting the sexy back in marriage. Susie Davis's style is as comfortable as a conversation over coffee with a best friend—and like a friend, she's unafraid to ask tough questions. This is not simply a book about sex—it's a thoughtful and brave look at making your marriage truly healthy. I'm ready to take the challenge."

Ronne
Married to Brad for 13 years

"I loved Susie's practical approach to marriage, the humorous stories, and the insightful comments from REAL husbands on their REAL views and needs. This is a fantastic read . . . not only for those struggling in their marriage, but also those who already have a great marriage. . . . Susie has managed to combine great instruction, gentle reminders, and lots of laughs in between. After I finished the book, my husband picked it up and also could not stop reading until he finished the book. He commented that it was the best advice to women he has ever heard . . . and coming from a man, that says it all!"

Joni
Married to Kevin for 13 years

"*Uncovered* sparked a fire in me that I didn't even know had gone out. This book has changed my attitude and my approach toward my husband. After reading the first chapter, I was motivated to lean over and give my husband a passionate kiss. He responded by asking, 'Is this a step by step book?' No, it's better. It's a reminder that my husband is truly longing for just one thing—me."

Julie
Married to David for 14 years

"I thought I had a good marriage, but after reading this book I know I can have a GREAT marriage! Lots of easy, practical concepts that I am already implementing. My life is busy as a mother of four boys, but I now realize my husband needs to be my priority AND I want my boys to see how a wife should treat her husband! I need to be an example for my sons of what a good wife looks like."

Beth
Married to Barry for 20 years

"*Uncovered* gave me a renewed passion for my husband and was a great reminder of why I fell in love with him in the first place. Every man should buy this book for his wife. . . . It will make for a VERY happy home."

Christy
Married to David for 15 years

"Susie uses her uniquely funny and real-world style to make women take an honest look at our lives and priorities. *Uncovered* is a refreshing reminder that my husband deserves more than my 'left-overs' at the end of the day. The reality is, being in tune and responsive to each other physically has great benefits for both of us!"

Holly
Married to Gary for 23 years

"*Uncovered* is funny, insightful, and full of common sense. *Uncovered* refreshed, rejuvenated, and reminded me what kind of wife I wanted to be, even after 22 years of marriage!"

Liz
Married to Steve for 22 years

"*Uncovered* has brought new energy to my thoughts and feelings about my husband. The entertaining and practical tips on spiritual, emotional, and physical communication really work. I feel freer in all areas of relating in my marriage, and we both benefit from the results!"

Jodi
Married to Erick for 19 years

"As I read *Uncovered*, I was encouraged to find that the differences my husband and I experience are not unique to our marriage. With humor and insight, Susie gives practical steps to make my marriage better. I left the book feeling excited about the future of my marriage. I am not only eager to share this book with friends in my stage in life, but also think it is a must read for those just starting out."

Julie
Married to Sam for 22 years

Uncovered

REVEALING THE SECRETS
OF A SEXY MARRIAGE

Susie Davis

Revell
a division of Baker Publishing Group
Grand Rapids, Michigan

Published by Revell
a division of Baker Publishing Group
P.O. Box 6287, Grand Rapids, MI 49516-6287
www.revellbooks.com

Printed in the United States of America

Library of Congress Cataloging-in-Publication Data
Davis, Susie, 1963–
    Uncovered : revealing the secrets of a sexy marriage / Susie Davis.
      p.   cm.
    Includes bibliographical references.
    ISBN 978-0-8007-3392-6 (pbk.)
    1. Sex—Religious aspects—Christianity. 2. Marriage—Religious aspects—
Christianity. I. Title.
    BT708.D384 2010
    248.8′435—dc22   2010001466

10   11   12   13   14   15   16   7   6   5   4   3   2   1

To my husband, Will Davis Jr.—
for twenty-five years of marriage . . .
and for sharing all kinds of fabulous little secrets.

Contents

Acknowledgments

Thanks to . . .

- Will Davis Jr.—my husband and my best friend
- Will III, Emily, and Sara—amazing people who just happen to be my kids
- Dee Ehlers—editor and friend extraordinaire
- Lynn Walker, Christy May, Jodi Allen, Kalli Smith, Erin Aspegren, Julie Washington, Carol Young, Kristi Vaught, Liz Benigno, Melissa Patterson, Stephanie Lucke, Jeanne Crosno, Joni and Kevin Kendrick, Gary Sinclair, Todd Lewis, Richard Hasting, Mike Helton, Gary Walsh, Tony Colvin, and Blake Ehlers—for wisdom, humor, and authenticity
- Bill Jensen—for merciless teasing, expounding, and agenting
- Revell—my marvelous publisher led by the fabulous Baker boys
- Lonnie Hull DuPont—for believing in a girl, a book, and a title that occasionally colors outside the lines

- Claudia Marsh—for being an outstanding publicist, dining with us on the Riverwalk, and putting us on the whiteboard
- Deonne Beron—for carting us around Michigan in the freezing cold and introducing me to the best chai tea latte on the planet
- Carmen Pease, Twila Bennett, Janelle Mahlmann—for endless marketing of Davis books
- Barb Barnes—for kind, light editing that makes me smile

The Male Room Revealed

The Male Room* section of the book is fairly simple. Since much of what I am writing about is in regard to what men think or say, I figured it would be more compelling if I got responses from real, live men. I knew that if I had actual men respond to the chapter themes, that would increase your likelihood of believing and agreeing to go along with my suggestions.

What I did was create a team of guys. These guys love their wives and honor their marriages. They keep lust in check and don't feed on pornography. And besides that, they've all been married at least a decade. They're businessmen: contractors, salesmen, CEOs, and ministers. They represent your everyman—the guy next door.

So here's how it worked: After I finished writing each chapter, I sent several of the married men some questions. I didn't let them read the chapters—so they had no idea what

---

*Names have been changed to protect the innocent! If I used their real names here, you'd be stalking them either in love or hate—and I just couldn't do that to them, bless their sweet, manly hearts!

I had written—I simply sent them the questions cold. And then they answered via email. The very first round was for the chapter titled "Is Food the New Sex?" and the responses I got were so fabulous. The men were incredibly honest in their responses. But when the time came for me to see them, they were funny about letting me read what they had written. This is an email I got from one of the guys:

> Susie,
> Is this a joke? Are you secretly trying to figure out if your husband is the only one that thinks about sex all the time? I must say the excuse of writing a book is a very creative way to find out. See my answers below.
> You're not gonna kick me out of the church for answering honestly are you?

What's not to love about that? They are such a great group of guys.

Back to the explanation. Their answers are uncut. I didn't pretty them up or move the sentences around. The only thing I corrected, if need be, was the grammar or spelling. The answers you read at the end of the chapters are the raw, real responses from those men. Men whom I think you will grow to appreciate—for their honesty is vulnerable. And what they have to say is touching. But mainly, it's just incredibly helpful. Some of their responses may be just what your husband would say if he had been asked.

I'm thinking that their responses will ignite your curiosity about what your husband thinks about these issues. And I'm hoping that perhaps you'll enter into dialogue with him about what you're reading. But mostly, I'm praying that you'll read this book and be drawn with an irresistible, undeniable compulsion to love your husband body and soul. That you'll become the wife you know your man needs, and that you'll have the marriage you've always dreamed of—with the man of your dreams.

Introduction

My garage is a mess. Cobwebs hang dutifully in the corners, boxes and bags of who knows what hide behind bikes, and a dusty old refrigerator sits sullen and quiet. I know my garage is dirty. I know that it needs organizing and sanitizing. Every day that I walk through it to get in my car, it begs for my immediate attention.

So I am going to pray about it. And after I pray about it, I am going to google "garage organization and cleanliness." Then I'll probably participate in a neighborhood support group for people like me who have trouble with their garages too. I am certain that is the best way to get to the bottom of my issues with my garage.

Ridiculous, right? And yet, in many ways, that is precisely how we approach a marriage that's become messy. We recognize that our marriage needs attention and send up an SOS prayer. We read online articles that delve into the issues married couples face. And sometimes, we even join a self-help group and listen to others expound on their problems.

Now don't get me wrong, I believe there is a place for prayer, research, and therapy (been there, done that, and reaped the benefit). It's just that I think the truth is that while many of us are motivated to better our ho-hum marriages, we spend all our time and energy becoming experts on the subject without actually ever *doing anything.*

Never before have we had more information at our fingertips, and nonetheless, we are still confounded. We live in the age of information, yet that has done little to fix some of our most stubborn cultural problems—debt, obesity, divorce.

This is a book designed to help you *do something* about your marriage. Tucked away in the pages are surefire tips to fix your marriage. Today. As a matter of fact, I think no matter what the state of your marriage, you can "quick fix" it and turn it into something wonderful with that man you love.

Now if you're like most people, something inside of you is railing against the idea that there is a quick fix for something as complex as a marriage relationship. And while it is true there are some issues that take professional guidance, such as a marriage fraught by sexual addiction or abuse, the majority of marriages just need a kick-start in the right direction. If you are committed to your marriage and still feel even occasional tenderness toward your spouse, this is just the book for you. As a matter of fact, if you read and implement only half of the suggestions, I can promise you'll have a happier marriage.

So before you read even one more word, I ask you to pledge that you will *do at least half of the suggestions in this book.* (Honestly, if you'll just add a little speed sex to your marriage you could probably stop at that one.) But even if you can't promise now, please know that because you haven't closed this book yet and you are reading this intro—you are already that much closer to actually doing something to improve your marriage.

And all you need to do right now is just turn the page— that will give you the jump-start you need to improve your relationship with the most important person in your life.

But you'll never know until you try . . .

1
Speed Sex

MORE IS BETTER AND IT DOESN'T HAVE TO LAST FOREVER

It's always amusing to read about new studies that come out with "findings" that are incredibly obvious. Like just last year when the newspapers and periodicals were aflurry with the report from a team of sex therapists. The exciting new report in the *Journal of Sexual Medicine* concluded that the optimum time for intercourse was three to thirteen minutes. This, apparently, was groundbreaking news for the researchers. They gathered 1,500 couples, armed the women with stopwatches, and asked them to gauge how long it took to have mutually satisfying sex. The study concluded that the median time was 7.3 minutes, dispelling the belief that "if you really want to satisfy your partner, you should last forever."[1]

Last forever . . . are they kidding? First off, that's a myth of male proportions promulgated in men's locker rooms. Second, who has that kind of time? My girlfriends and I are busy, busy women; we don't want to have a man who's not interested in getting things going on. If indeed we did—wait around for the perfect, longest-lasting moment the sex therapist team seems to be thinking that we want to have—our dear husbands simply wouldn't get any at all.

For goodness' sake, when my kids were toddlers, by the time they were tucked into bed and right before my head hit the pillow, there were truly only a few viable moments when sex sounded even vaguely appealing. I was so wiped out that if my husband thought about making things *last forever*, I would have politely refused, opting for sleep instead. Then fast-forward a few, and we've got a houseful of teenagers—we both just wish for a time when we can outlast their night-owl tendencies. Or hope they'll stay in the shower long enough for us to catch a quickie before they get out of the bathroom.

> It doesn't take long to satisfy a woman in bed. A survey of sex therapists concluded the optimal amount of time for sexual intercourse was 3 to 13 minutes. The findings, to be published in the May issue of the Journal of Sexual Medicine, strike at the notion that endurance is the key to a great sex life.[2]

Whatever happened to the quickie, by the way? You'd think that the researchers would have heard of that one. I know all my girlfriends have. They're those tiny moments that married couples regard as golden opportunities. Little snippets of time devoted to reconnecting sexually. Women know that it takes some serious creativity to manage not only setting at least a semi-sizzling mood but securing some privacy as well. Whether an afternoon quickie in bed (and making it up in time so that the kids aren't suspicious), in the closet (I have one girlfriend who says her walk-in is the default location), or in the shower (lock that bathroom door)—the wives I know are masters of what I call speed sex.

Step-by-Step Speed Sex

Let me start by telling you what speed sex is not. It's not just "servicing" a man. And it's not about settling for unsatisfying sex. And it's not about checking sex off a long to-do list. It's not about that at all. It is, however, a pragmatic approach to marital sex. It's about being creative and thoughtful. It's about being available and responsive. It's about understanding the truth about sex: that sex is a really big deal in marriage . . . and it should be. It's about realizing that if you intend to have a healthy physical relationship with your husband, then you might need to find creative, spontaneous, and yes, sometimes even speedy ways to approach the thing. I have to be honest here: I think understanding and utilizing speed sex could revolutionize your marriage. But I'm certainly not going to make any promises that you aren't willing to keep.

One: Sex Is a Big Deal Because God Made It That Way

The first step in getting friendly with the speed sex approach is to realize the importance of sex in marriage. It's not just about baby making and it's not just for pleasure either. In *Intimate Issues* by Linda Dillow and Lorraine Pintus, the authors outline six key reasons sex is truly a gift from God. I really like their list and wholeheartedly agree with them. So, are you ready? Here we go:

God made sex to create life.
God made sex for intimate oneness.
God made sex for personal, physical knowledge of one another.
God made sex for pleasure.
God made sex as a defense against temptation.
And finally, God made sex for comfort.[3]

To me, that list goes back and forth like waves hitting the beach. Life. Oneness. Knowledge. Pleasure. Defense. Comfort. The amazing love expression spoken between a husband and wife. You've got to admit, God did a fabulous thing in

17

creating sex, and he was pure genius to keep it within the framework of the covenant of marriage. There's no place better to appreciate the vulnerability, the nakedness—physically, emotionally, and spiritually.

Now, maybe you understand the importance of sex, but you just don't feel it. And you don't feel like doing anything about it. Well, you're not alone. Many women are the same way. As a matter of fact, psychiatrist Anita Clayton says that while men regard dissatisfaction in the bedroom as a crisis, women simply settle for less.[4] Maybe you've been there, done that—after a long day's work, you succumb to the overtures from your husband without feeling any connection at all. And then you end up feeling as though you simply settled for less. It's a common occurrence, but one that, given some needed perspective, doesn't have to be.

Perhaps settling for less is a result of women failing to understand the aforementioned list. Just maybe, we've fallen prey to thinking of sex as just physical—like what we see portrayed in the media—and we've failed to remember that sex is much more than physical. It's emotional and spiritual too.

Let's take the "God made sex for comfort" angle. I believe on many levels we as women miss the comfort associated with sex because we're always thinking that sex is just about pleasure (or nonpleasure). And we erroneously think that sex has nothing to do with acting as a balm for those things that bother us emotionally. So instead of seeking comfort through intimacy with our husbands, we look to food or new shoes. It's as if somewhere way deep inside we get the whole idea of physicality bringing solace to our psyches through "comfort food" and "retail therapy," but we miss the physicality of capturing solace through sex.

If you think about it honestly and without any predisposition, you have to agree that God hardwired us for sex. And when you realize that he included in that the ability *to seek and to find* certain things through physical intimacy with our husbands, it can turn the tide. One of those avenues is comfort. God designed us to receive deep, emotional comfort through sex. If you have a hard time believing me, try it. Next time you feel sad, instead of opening the pantry, find your husband. Tell him that you're perplexed and bothered—and that you need some contact for comfort. It might seem counterintuitive, but why not try it? It's step number one in this whole speed sex approach . . . being open to the idea that sex is a big deal in marriage—and that quite possibly, you haven't even begun to discover all the fabulousness of it.

> *Couples develop sexual problems when they both view sex as merely a physical thing. Both of them need to use their creativity to make it a more fulfilling experience.*[5]
>
> Dr. Kevin Leman

Two: You Are a Red-Hot Mama Whether or Not You Know It Yet

And that brings me to the second thing about speed sex . . . the more you do it, the more you like it, and the better it gets. Studies have shown that the more you engage physically and sexually, the more likely you will want to engage—and the more enjoyable it will become. As unbelievable as it might seem, in the words of author Lorilee Craker,

You are a red-hot mama whether or not you know it yet. And once you let that hot side of you free, she'll revitalize you in ways you never dreamed of. Because the truth of the matter is, great sex energizes rather than depletes you. It conveys love and affection, soothes, comforts, and relaxes, and relieves stress outside and inside your relationship. Passion bridges the gap when the inevitable conflicts flare, and it enhances closeness. Most of all, when that red-hot mama inside of you is activated, you are reminded that you're more than a meat-cutting, squabble-settling, sock-matching robot. You become playful, flirty, and sensual, the way God created you to be.[6]

I love Lori's words there. And I really want to be "playful, flirty, and sensual." But in so many ways being "red hot" and being a "mama" seem worlds apart. I think it's because the phrase seems like such an oxymoron. Think about it, "red hot" and "mama" don't really fit together nicely, do they? And yet, the "red hot" part was exactly what made you a "mama" in the first place.

For me and many women I know, it's difficult to disengage from the mama/mothering aspect. Partly because it's an all-consuming, all-encompassing job. And partly because being a mother and being a hottie seem to be diabolically opposed to one another. When I envision a "mama," I see a sweet, doelike woman cuddling an infant at her breast. When I envision "red hot," I see a cleavage-filled, tank-top-wearing twenty-one-year-old poured into some teeny, tiny ripped-up jeans. The two visuals couldn't be more dissimilar. But I don't think they have to be.

I'm not really sure why we go from seemingly surrendering our whole selves to our husbands to doing an about-face and surrendering our whole selves to our children—not sure at all. But in truth, I see it all the time. A woman who once had been the cutest, sexiest new bride becomes, in just a matter of years, the cutest, unsexiest little mommy. It's strangely backward but incredibly recurrent. Author Caitlin Flanagan suggests that perhaps it's because "once children come along, it's easy for parents to regard each other as copresidents of an industrious little corporation."[7] And yes, I agree. But who did the duping and got us to believe that we can't actually be a sexy little wife and run a successful household complete with kids? Sexy may be redefined as we age, but it's not gone altogether! I think we need not give up without a fight. Because when we surrender the sexy part of our femininity exclusively to childrearing, we are giving away a piece that is rightfully ours as a woman and a wife. And if we're really honest here, we're giving away a piece that is rightfully our husband's too.

Three: Your Man Is Priority One

I don't have to tell you that you're busy. Women today do it all and then some. We work at home, at work, at church, and at the kids' school. We volunteer, serve, drive, and do the dishes. It's amazing to me to think of all the "people" I've become. There's Susie the wife, the mom, the sister, the daughter, the friend, the author, the radio host, the speaker, the housekeeper, the horseback rider, the gardener, the reader, the employee, the employer, the church volunteer, the carpool driver, the decorator, the dietitian, the personal shopper, the laundress, the bill payer . . . the list goes on and on. It's likely as long as yours. And if you're anything like me, you're having great difficulty shortening it and equal difficulty managing each role with excellence. Maybe now is the time to do some hardcore prioritizing. Ready?

Priority number one: the man. Your man. I'm talking just plain and simple, *priority one is the man you married.* He didn't marry you because you were a great mom, sister, daughter, friend . . . you get the drift. He married you because you were plain and simple *a fabulous, sensual woman.* Yes, take a breath, dear, of course he loves "your personality and your heart" but let's get real. He looked at you and he saw lips, breasts, curvy hips, bodacious booty—you know, all that.

Now don't despair if you feel as though somehow you've grown cold or lost yourself along the way. The heat isn't too difficult to reignite. But don't just sit around waiting for it. William Butler Yeats said, "Do not wait to strike till the iron is hot; but make it hot by striking it."[8] Couldn't agree more. So let's just get to the heart of what it takes to strike the iron.

What to do? Take time for sexy you. Stop worrying about all that needs to get done and rediscover who it was that

21

caught that man in the first place. Where did she go? Or shall I say . . . when did she let it all go?

Four: Rediscover Sensual, Sexy You

If you're reading and realizing that you probably need to recover some of the sizzle but aren't sure where to find it, I have good news. Because I'm going to outline a few of the things that I think we routinely miss as modern women. In the spin of living our busy lives, there are a few basic tips that could point you in the right direction to getting your sexy back.

First off, get around your girlfriends who act and talk like women—not just mommies. I have a couple friends who are so good about this. They love their husbands and boy, oh boy, do their husbands love them. One friend of mine has a (minimum) three times a week sex commitment with her man. She does not fuss or cuss or make excuses—she is committed to sex three times a week no matter what. And she's not chained to the bed or dragging around tired all day. She's got a full-time job, a spotless house, and two teenagers—and a very devoted, satisfied husband I might add. Another girlfriend is always after the latest and greatest new thing for her face and body. She's the Sephora Queen—smells yummy. Looks fabo. She's young, cute, and sexy at fortysomething without being overdone. And she is always talking about creative ways to seduce her man. I have, on many occasions, appreciated her candor and tips. She's a real original—a sexy

> The rare and enviable woman is not the one liberated enough to tell hurtful secrets about her marriage to her girlfriends or the reading public. Nor is she the one capable of attracting the sexual attentions of a variety of worthy suitors. The rare woman—the good wife, the happy one—is the woman who maintains her husband's sexual interest and who returns it in full measure.[9]
>
> Caitlin Flanagan

mother of two with a big old house and a ton of extended family to care for . . . and yet, she always has her husband on her mind. I like that.

Second, do something with your body. Discover your strength again. Get out there and move. Ride, walk, run, swim, stretch, and then get a massage. One of the best things Will ever did for me (and for him coincidentally) was gift me with a horseback riding lesson for my birthday. I rode horses as a child but had to stop because of finances, and so for my thirty-first, he gave me private instructions with a trainer. Over a decade later, I still ride—usually three times a week. And I have to say that not only has it kept me out of a therapist's office, it has given me the capacity I need to stay connected with my body physically. When I ride, it reminds me that I can use my body to do things that are amazing and surprising—

It's all right letting yourself go, as long as you can get yourself back.[10]

regardless of how many babies I've had or how tired my skin has become. I am still strong and agile and able. That translates well if you know what I mean.

Finally, find your inner hippie. Make peace with yourself. Stop striving and fighting to get your whole world in order and just *relax*. Take a deep breath and peace out, sister. It's all going to get done one way or another—and if it doesn't, is that such a traumatic thing anyway? Is it worth being so dead tired that you can't even think of having sex with your husband? I truly believe that part of recovering the sensual side in you is in taking time to smell the roses, so to speak. There is something amazingly sensual about having a relaxed attitude about life.

So I say unleash the sensual. You can do it easy enough. For example, take some time this evening and find some grooving music to listen to while making dinner. Turn it up and sing it out. Better yet, let loose and do some "who cares" dancing before embarking on that dinner prep. If that sounds

23

too wild and weird, then quiet it down a little. How about building a roaring fire, finding a cozy spot, and toasting those toesies? Whichever suits you, unwind for a few precious moments and rediscover the sensual parts of your life. Then linger over your dinner and truly enjoy the texture and taste of your food. Remember and possibly relearn how to savor life's everyday experiences with an appreciation for how it impacts your senses.

For me, getting outside brings me down a notch. Maybe you could consider developing a serious outdoor habit. Whether it's exercising or gardening or swinging in a hammock and reading a book—get your mind and body outside. (If you're really free, you could invest in a private outdoor shower like one of my hippie girlfriends.) Let the sun sit on your skin. Feel the wind play with your hair. Lie down on the grass and then look up at that big blue sky and realize . . . someone made you. And that someone made the whole amazing universe. He certainly didn't expect you not to drink in the goodness through your senses, whether in your backyard or with your husband. Enjoy the gift—and in doing so, reconnect with your Creator God because he is the one who can truly lead you to finding the sensual side that you (and your husband) might be missing.

Want to be crazy sexy with your husband? Then start to experience again (or perhaps for the first time) the amazing delight of being a sensual woman.

Uncovering the Truth

- *Be totally honest here: how long does it take to have "optimal" sex? If you honestly have no idea—then next time check the clock. Probably not near the time you think it takes.*

- *When you think of how little time is at stake for such a big issue as sex, does it surprise you that you would dismiss your husband's advances? What do you think is really behind saying no to sex?*

- *Without looking at the list, see if you can name the six reasons God made sex. (Check the list if you can't remember.) After reviewing the list, see if you can remember having sex for all six reasons. What do you think is the reason you most often have sex? How about your husband? Could you be brilliantly brave and ask your husband about his perspective regarding the list?*

- *Are you the same sensual woman your husband married? If not, why not?*

- *What are a few steps you can take to rediscovering your sexy you?*

THE MALE ROOM:
Responses from Real Men Who Love Their Wives

What caught your eye the first time you saw the woman who would become your wife?

BARRY: Physically, it was her general attractiveness—she wasn't a blond bombshell but it was clear that she was confident of herself and her body. She was trim, dressed nicely, and made you look a second time. More generally, I was also attracted to her interest and ability to talk about things that meant something—her relationship with God, family, children, the church—along with everyday things that most of us enjoy conversing about as well.

JOHN: Her kindness, seriously. I didn't even consider her since she was ten years younger than me. I was divorced, balding, and had a daughter. She was twenty-two and dating some of the most handsome men in town.

BEN: She was drop-dead gorgeous and was totally righteous. She was the best of both worlds.

DAVE: To be honest, it was her purity. She was young, absolutely beautiful, humble, and complete. She wasn't trying to *be* something or *look* a certain way or even trying to catch anyone's eye, she was simply her. I can still see her in my mind's eye just as if she was standing before me now—and I still get chill bumps.

Looking at the list below of six reasons God made sex, which motivates you most often?

God made sex to create life.

God made sex for intimate oneness.

God made sex for personal, physical knowledge of one another.

God made sex for pleasure.

God made sex as a defense against temptation.

God made sex for comfort.

JOHN: The pleasure of sexual desire.

BEN: For pleasure.

BARRY: God made sex for intimate oneness. While there are (were) certainly times when the other items on the list come into play, this one is really prominent for us most often. Maybe it's because of being "busy" a lot that while it certainly brings pleasure, sex is a reminder and statement that we both still matter to each other and that our true closeness is for one another, no one else.

DAVE: God made sex for intimate oneness.

What or who would you say is your wife's number one top priority?

BEN: Her relationship with God.

JOHN: No question, her children.

BARRY: Apart from God, I would say me. She is loyal almost to a fault. I'm pretty lucky that way. She would tell you she's definitely a golden retriever, and I no doubt take advantage of that some of the time.

DAVE: Fixing my fashion sense. She's been working on it for twenty-two years now and has finally convinced me to give up tube socks. It's not the teacher's fault, I'm a poor student. Seriously, I'd say her priority is serving God in whatever way he sets before her. I've never seen a more pure servant's heart. It has made me more of a servant than I would have ever been otherwise.

Be totally honest here, how long does it take to have "optimal sex"?

JOHN: I would say optimal sex for my wife is around five to ten minutes. My optimal is generally three to five minutes after that. Tell me if I have this all wrong and I just embarrassed myself.

BEN: Twenty minutes.

DAVE: A few years ago my answer would have been different, but as we age we learn that anything lasting longer than 4 hours needs a doctor's attention. I'd say at least a half hour. Take time to enjoy and relish in it. Then take time to recover. As I age the relish time is shorter and shorter and the recover time is longer and longer!

BARRY: The median time from our years of record-keeping is 9.4 minutes not aided by the wind. Seriously, I would say 20–30 minutes.

2

Is Food the New Sex?

HOW THINKING LIKE A MAN CAN CREATE A CRAVING

Food is the new sex . . . at least that's what the headline reads. I'm sitting here perusing a thought-provoking essay by Mary Eberstadt about our national attitudes toward food and sex. It's an interesting premise she proposes—that we "have taken long-standing morality about sex and substituted it onto food. The all you can eat buffet is now stigmatized and the sexual smorgasbord is not."[1] And that we are subsequently left with "mindful eating and mindless sex" that creates a whole new set of rules and a heightened moral fervor where our food choices are concerned. Agreeably—she may be on to something. But honestly, I am more interested in something that she didn't propose. The possibility that, quite literally for some married women, preparing, serving, and enjoying food has become a substitute for sex itself.

If you're honest about it, I think you'd agree that most people are obsessed with food in one way or another. It occupies a preeminent place in our minds and emotions. We talk about, plan, and schedule what, when, and where we are going to eat. We eat to celebrate and we eat for comfort.

We plan social events around food and we raid the fridge late at night. If we're dieting, we grumble about what we can't eat—and if we're not on a diet, we feel guilty about how much we are eating. It's all about food, glorious food. We're flooded with plentiful options (who doesn't love the Cooking Channel?) and constant availability. We can order our groceries online and have them delivered to our front door—yet we can't seem to get enough, and we just can't stop talking about it.

But not always so with sex in marriage. As a matter of fact, in *The Sex-Starved Marriage*, author Michele Weiner-Davis cites research that indicates one in twenty couples are making love fewer than ten times a year.[2] And even in marriages where sex is operational, many times there just seems to be a deadly serious lack of desire and enthusiasm. Seems we're just tired. (*Ho-hum, yawn*—excuse me.) Whether it's a sudden headache or a stressed-out schedule, more often than once in a while we utter a "Not tonight, honey" and ask for a pass. But not so with the chips and salsa or a big bowl of Ben & Jerry's ice cream, you know? I know I'm never too tired to eat. But sex? Well . . . that just depends. And truthfully, my girlfriends seem to agree. But the preference on that whole dynamic is somewhat curious, and though I've yet to untangle the whole psychology of it, I do know this: the married men I know are honestly quite frustrated by it. As a matter of fact, when surveying for this book, I found the one complaint men had most often was their wives' apparent boredom and apathy in the bedroom.

Women in a committed relationship lose their sex drives much sooner than their male partners, says a new German study. A survey by sex researcher Dietrich Klusman found that after four years in a steady relationship, most women reported a sharp drop in their interest in having regular intercourse. As for men, their libido hardly dented, even after 40 years of marriage.[3]

Meet Me at The Cheesecake Factory

I read an article in *Newsweek* recently asserting that women have greater difficulty than men saying no to choice food items. In a piece entitled "Weight Loss: Why Guys Don't Diet the Way Women Do," writer Kurt Soller reports:

> Earlier this year, the Brookhaven National Laboratory conducted a study where they presented male and female subjects their favorite foods, then monitored their brain activity. Ladies, the gents beat you: they were able to suppress their hunger and their desire to eat, while brain activity among the women showed that many continued to crave their favorite foods, even after being told to think of something else. In layman's terms, we call this "emotional eating," something that trainer and American Dietetic Association spokesman Jim White says is an "uphill battle" for his female clients, but not the male ones. The guys must be too busy thinking of something else—or nothing at all?[4]

I thought it was quite humorous that the writer proposed two options for what men were thinking about: something else or nothing at all. And yes, I believe it's true—they are definitely busy thinking of something else. And it isn't a menu option at The Cheesecake Factory. While women are thinking of food, men are thinking about sex. And to the extent women are obsessing about food, men are obsessing about sex. Sex, not food, is the thing that creates an uphill battle for men. It's what they think about and desire even when denied. While guys may be better able to say no to delicious foods and move on—they don't seem to have equal success in turning off their sexual hunger. So in a sense, sex is the "food" men think of most.

It's easy to see how food and sex create similar longings—they're both so sensual and desirable. When fully enjoyed, both involve all five of our senses, release pleasure endorphins, and culminate in a state of well-being and relaxation. Of course, the problem is that men and women are seeking a sensual feast

31

in two different places. But I am convinced that we women are missing the boat on this one. While cooking and eating are fun and satisfying, the primary role of food is physical nourishment. It is not meant to be an emotional or relational connector. Sex, on the other hand, was created for just that purpose.

The physical intimacy your husband craves with you is his most significant way to connect with you. Psychologist Dr. Kevin Leman explains:

> What's the #1 need for a man in marriage? Affirmation? It's important, but not the top need. Communication? Get real! Sex? Now you're talking . . . but this isn't exactly right either. Most women think that most men are "after only one thing," but that's far too simplistic. The #1 need is not sex, but *sexual fulfillment*. That's a heck of a difference. A man's sexual need is far more than just physical. It's also mental and, believe it or not, emotional. A lot of wives don't realize this about their husbands. (Frankly, a lot of husbands don't realize this about themselves.) Couples develop sexual problems when they both view sex as merely a physical thing. Both of them need to use their creativity to make it a more fulfilling experience.[5]

As unbelievable as it may seem, connecting with you in bed is your husband's ultimate cheesecake lunch event and then some.

Now, I'm no therapist. I'm not going to expound on all the possible underlying reasons women seem more excited about joining girlfriends for lunch than meeting their husbands for a rendezvous, but I can offer some intriguing tips for the woman who is interested in reversing this trend in her marriage and regaining at least some of her lost sexual desire for her husband.

Create a Craving

Think back to the study about women and food. The women continued to crave the food even after being told to think of something else. They showed an inability to disengage. If you're an average female, you know exactly what that feels like. Let's say you're on a low-carb diet so you've denied yourself your favorite foods for several days. It's not getting easier and every day you are faced with seeing and smelling the fabulousness of bread and pasta and chips and cookies. It seems like *everybody* except you always has something delish and carbo rich right at their lips. And it's driving you *crazy*. If you've been there, done that, then you know the essence of craving. Now, what I'd like you to do is transfer that kind of craving onto your sex life. I want you to try and think about sex like your husband does.

Before you write me off as weird or get all out of whack, consider again that while eating might be an uphill battle for you, your husband (should he be an average man) is experiencing an uphill battle in the sexual arena. He's thinking about sex many more times than you (perhaps as much as you are thinking about ripping into that loaf of French bread) and that's creating an immense personal struggle for him. So if you're willing to try and put yourself in his shoes, the effects could be revolutionary.

Here's where the fun comes in. The starting point for creating a sexual craving is really not difficult. For the next week just determine to start thinking about sex with your man as often as possible. It could be as simple as not turning off the thoughts that already cross your mind and going with the flow. But I bet if you're like most women, you might need a little more of a challenge. So what I'd like you to do is commit to trying to think about sex as often as you think your husband does. If you don't know how much your husband thinks about sex, you could be a brave girl and ask him. Or you can just take my word for it that it's *at least* double how often you think of it. Either way, the goal is to intentionally add the thoughts to your mental pattern. You might think all this sounds crazy—or impossible—but it's not.

It's kind of like when you're having a dinner party—if you're having ten people over for dinner next weekend I certainly don't have to remind you to think about getting ready for it. You're excited and looking forward to the event. You naturally go about your busy day with thoughts about the evening continually running through your mind. You create a menu. And you keep a list close by of things you want to buy at the grocery store. You write down a list of things to do to prep the house for your guests. You drive through traffic, imagining how you will set the table with flowers and which side dishes go best with the entrée. You think about how to distract the kids when everyone starts arriving. When you get back home, you make a mental note that the porch needs sweeping and the trash needs to be taken out. It's as if anything and everything is prompting you to think of your party.

> God made men the way they are; men have hormones and urges. I believe that too many women think that men are over-sexed, but in this area men are not self-made. For men, it does not take a super sex partner to keep a man happy. Making love with the wife, even at low frequency, keeps a man healthy and home.[6]
>
> Anonymous male

Well, that's just the sort of mental exercise I'm asking you to do in regard to your man and your marriage—to start thinking about and getting ready for your next sexual encounter. If it helps, schedule it in your calendar and start a to-do list. Imagine the event, plan for it, and yes, fantasize about the whole deal. In the same way that you see the table set for your dinner party, visualize the scene with your man. (Hello—it's completely legal with your husband!) Anything and everything to get your mind set on creating a craving for your husband. He's changing his shirt in the closet—you think, *Wow, biceps. Cute.* He's clean and fresh smelling as he walks out the door—you think, *That's all mine.* He calls to check in at noon—you think, *Don't know how I got so lucky to have that thoughtful man.* You're running errands, picking up his clothes at the dry cleaners—you think, *He looks so hot and handsome in those khakis and a starched white shirt.* He comes in tired and worn at the end of a day—you think, *So glad to have that hardworking, irresistible man home.*

Marabel Morgan, author of *The Total Woman*, claims, "A woman's most important sex organ is her brain."[7] And I couldn't agree with her more. It's your thoughts that create the impetus for action. Thinking about being with your husband sexually, thinking about the physical, sensual part of your relationship—that's what will create more of the craving. (Hey, you might even skip that dinner and plan a little party for just the two of you.)

Mental Exercises in How to Think Like a Man (or how about just understanding what a man is thinking . . .)

Now, since I'm not a man, you might not believe what I'm telling you. So you actually might disbelieve that your man really thinks about sex all that often. I could tell you that research bears it out. An ABC news poll found that the majority of men think about sex every day. And that's double the rate among women. Statistically, 43 percent of men think about sex several times a day while only 13 percent of women do.[8] But even with that, you might not believe me. If you've never had an honest conversation with your husband, you may think he thinks about sex only as often as you have it. (Ha!)

So in order to convince you that he really does think about sex more often than you—and to convince you that those kinds of

> *When sex is withheld, the need for and lack of it becomes a constant state of mind for men. It forces men to turn their thoughts outward. I believe that most men would not settle for a fast-food burger when they have prime rib at home, but when they are hungry, they will find a way to get fed. I believe that most men do not want to leave their wives—they are driven out by a lack of physical love, compassion, and understanding in the area of sexuality.[9]*
>
> Anonymous male

thought patterns are actually normal for healthy guys—I've done something different at the end of this chapter. I have asked my whole team from The Male Room to answer the questions.

Here's my thinking: I am hoping you believe me when I say that these are great guys, committed to their wives and to covenant marriage. And I am hoping that their sometimes funny, sometimes touching, always honest answers will allow you to peek into the male mind—the happily married male mind. And that you'll realize that guys just think differently than women about sex. They think about it almost constantly. That's how they're wired, but it doesn't mean that they're perverts or oversexed. It just means they're guys.

My little exposé is not about startling or confusing you. In fact, it's just the opposite. It's meant to soothe and demystify what perhaps you still struggle to understand about your own husband. And in doing that, I am hoping to help you get to a point where you're able to . . . well, think more like a man for your man.

Uncovering the Truth

- *Be honest: how many times do you think about sex a day—or a week?*
- *Okay, now how many times do you think your husband thinks about sex a day—or a week?*
- *Is there evidence in your life that your mind is your most important sex organ? If yes, explain. If no, what does motivate you sexually?*
- *What are three things you can do to add the thought pattern to your daily life?*

THE MALE ROOM:
Responses from Real Men Who Love Their Wives

For lunch, would you prefer a really good cheeseburger or a rendezvous in bed with your wife?

JOHN: You're joking, right?

JACK: I am surprised you thought a silly cheeseburger might stand up to a nooner. Not even in the same universe.

CARSON: A cheeseburger, served in bed, with my wife is optimal. Okay . . . silly answer to a silly question. If my wife offered me a rendezvous where I didn't have to play games with wondering whether she was going to be open to the idea or not, I'd take that in a minute. If it is the burger versus the having to play the right part, walking on eggshells, wondering if she has changed the mating ritual this week and whether I will have the right ritual to impress the female, I'd rather have the burger. At least then I know where I stand.

MICHAEL: No hamburger could compete with a rendezvous with my wife.

BARRY: If you're suggesting that sometimes sex at "other" times than whatever is our normal is enjoyable, then I say yes. I think just being tired or having sex become somewhat repetitive is what takes at least some of the specialness out of it. I think the less we have a "normal" time the better. However, if you're suggesting giving up lunch every day? OK, I'll think about it.

BEN: First of all, cheeseburgers are bad for you. Second, the big, heavy lunch makes you sleepy and sluggish for the rest of the day. On the other hand, sex burns calories, invigorates you, and increases your life span. Sex wins. Any questions?

CHAD: I love cheeseburgers and sex (although not necessarily at the same time). I have turned down a cheeseburger meal but can't think of a time I have turned down a rendezvous

37

in bed with my wife . . . so I guess that wins out. Now that I have learned how to fast, I think that will further solidify sex over cheeseburgers.

JOSH: I'm a full believer that affection should never ever be used as currency. So with that out of the way, I'll take "rendezvous" for $1,000 please. Actually, she could name her price, but that isn't really something she needs to know, right? No doubt that the rendezvous would perk me up for the remaining part of the day, maybe even two days, but I'm all for a seven-day lunch program, so she'd never get me to admit a two-day value meal. She has been talking about the two of us getting into aerobics so I'm thinking that the heart-healthy aspect is a great selling point should the subject come up. Now I'm really thinking about this . . . heck, I might go an entire week without even thinking about a cheeseburger. That would make my doctor happy too. Not just me, but everybody is happier . . . my demeanor is up . . . this may have positive implications for the whole family and the office. I can hear it now: "Dad is so much happier and skinnier too." "You've been so productive this quarter working from home during lunch, so we are giving you a raise." If I'm to be totally honest, I would quite possibly schedule my entire day around it . . . I would forgo lunch altogether—burger or not—just to make certain that I was available. Talk about clock watching . . . it would be the longest morning ever! Okay, just thinking about the question has me rambling, I better stop here. In summary, between it being heart healthy to miss a burger and an unbelievably great idea that I haven't thought of more than ten thousand times (this month), I would definitely go with a rendezvous in bed with my wife over a really good cheeseburger. There!

DAVE: Any chance the rendezvous could include the cheeseburger? Seriously, lunch is good and all, but by comparison a cheeseburger isn't even good for you!

SAM: Are you kidding me? Rendezvous with my wife. Breakfast and dinner would be good too!

What time of day are you least likely to think about sex?

CHAD: When I am in a deep sleep for sure. The other least likely time would be when I am trying to get the four kids out the door to school in the morning. That's possibly one of the more miserable times of the day.

BARRY: Probably in the morning when the demands of the day are already percolating in my mind or any time we're simply exhausted.

MICHAEL: Midafternoon—the slump is all encompassing . . .

BEN: (Hopefully) when I'm reading the Bible and praying. Beyond that, it's fair game.

JOHN: While sleeping I don't have night dreams about sex, now daydreams are another thing altogether.

JOSH: First thing in the morning for sure. However if there was a planned, but missed, sexual encounter the night before then it would quite literally be the first thing I think of when I awake. And then it would be the dominant thing that I think about throughout the entire day and on into the next. This could go on for days. Thank God that my wife isn't passive-aggressive because it would certainly be a surefire way to torture the living daylights out of me. Oops, rambling again. Sorry.

JACK: Depends on what your definition of "day" is . . . 3:00 a.m.??

CARSON: At work.

SAM: Honestly, if there is a time and there really isn't, it would be between 4:30 and 6:00 p.m. when I'm the most tired, trying to unwind from the day and make the transition from work to dad to husband. Don't get me wrong though—I walk in the door and the kids are gone and my wife is ready, it'll raise the heart rate. That's the difference between men and women—men are ready to go no matter what's going on around us. We are multitaskers! :)

DAVE: That part of the day won't actually come true till we all meet in heaven . . . if then.

How much time elapses, during a typical day, between your thoughts about sex?

BEN: I think the smallest unit of time measurement discovered by science so far is the nanosecond. That would be close.

JACK: Have you ever tried to study with the radio on? Thinking about sex is kind of like good music continuously playing in the background . . . it's always on so you just learn to work around it.

CHAD: If I said once a day, then I would be lying. So let's just agree that guys are wired differently and any number of things can trigger a thought about sex during the day. I haven't tried counting and figure that would just be depressing. So I will hedge and say three—morning and night when I am in bed with my wife and when she gets out of the bath (I figure we are pretty close to naked at that point anyway).

CARSON: I've been married for twenty years now. I try really hard not to think about sex, because it is just frustrating to think about what you won't likely get. Sometimes I feel like I'm either too lazy or too beat down to do anything about it. And there doesn't appear to be anything I can do about it since my oath to God was a holy covenant to love, cherish, and honor my wife 'til death do us part. And death hasn't set in . . . yet. As repressed as I am, still maybe an hour or two between.

BARRY: That's a challenging question, because for men, if we're honest, we wrestle with temptation all the time, and that messes with our healthy, right thoughts about sex with our spouses. I wish that women in our culture understood that more about men in general. We're not all perverted (although we're all clearly tainted), but we are attracted by the visual, and many women simply don't get that in how they dress. The other complication is that I at least also find myself pondering a lot whether my wife is also interested at a given time. On the one hand, that's good, because I do want to be sensitive to her needs, time, and desires, but on the other hand, I can also simply avoid trying. So my answer is that

I think about it often (whatever that is) but on a variety of levels that are often complicated, messy, and challenging. I know I have learned to be less analytical over time. But hopefully there's still time for more maturing. Clear as mud, right?

MICHAEL: Not a—*sex*—whole—*sex*—lot—*sex sex sex*—of time.

JOHN: I question the word "thoughts." It's ambiguous for this kind of question regarding sex and men. Proactively thinking about sex is one thing; it's another thing for thoughts about sex to invade one's mind, then there are sexual "thoughts" as more of a "feeling" ever present throughout the day. Imagine it this way: when you're hungry yet preoccupied with life, at times you proactively think about eating. At other times the thought comes to you, "I should eat something," but if you think of it proactively, invasively, or not at all, the hunger is still there. In a sense the "thought" of sex is ever present.

JOSH: ANY thought about it at all??? I think that the record is 3 hours, but a typical day would be an hour. But then there are work days and nonwork days, and then there is that part of the day when I'm not working at all. Work is probably the number one hindrance to thinking about sex, so yep, a typical day would average to an hour or so.

DAVE: Enough time for me to make sure I am still breathing and acting as though I'm awake. Actually, I do sometimes spend a few moments thinking about old high school football glory that never really happened. Then back to sex.

SAM: I think I need a therapist!

3

Superman

Will and I have a long history of trouble with car travel. Put us in a plane together for miles on end, we're fine. But a car . . . well, that's a different story altogether. We just don't gel well on long trips when he's driving. He attributes the problem to a head-on collision I had four years ago. And that might be, because it was incredibly traumatic. A work van crossed four lanes of traffic and hit me head-on going sixty-five miles an hour. That'll mess with your mind and your face. So, yes, that might have something to do with it, but in addition, it might be his ADHD tendencies when he's driving. He'll be driving along taking a call and messing incessantly with his earpiece all the while trying to write stuff down and steer at the same time. He's somewhat like a puppy when he's driving—cute and fidgety. It's the fidgety part that touches my nerves.

So several years ago (in a moment of complete insanity) we decided that because of our budget, we'd drive instead of fly to his parents' cabin in Estes Park, Colorado, some thousand miles away. At 5:00 a.m., we packed up the Volvo wagon with the girls in the backseat and headed out for the big adventure. By the time we reached the highway about ten miles from our driveway, a distinct tightness developed in my chest, so I took several deep breaths hoping I'd relax. Will says I was sighing loudly—but in truth I honestly wanted to enjoy the road trip with my family. Will glanced my way. I smiled weakly. I grimaced. I was miserable. He kept driving, imagining that at some point I'd hit a high and enter nirvana. No such luck.

Suffice it to say that when the trip odometer hit mile 25 just outside Austin, Will performed one of his greatest man moments to date. Fed up with my "deep-breathing" exercises and excessive facial expressions, he pulled the car over in a teeny, tiny town called Seward Junction. And just as the car skidded to a stop on the gravel road, he said, "Susie, I love you but I'm turning around and taking you home. I am not driving all the way to Colorado like this. You and the girls can fly to Denver. Pick a flight, tell me what time, and I'll pick you up at the airport." And with that, he turned the car around and headed back to Austin. It happened so fast it made my head spin.

Caught off guard but adjusting rapidly, I rallied from my funk, realized what had happened, and begged him to stop driving back to Austin. Suddenly I was no longer worried about his driving or our safety or about the budget that got us there in the first place. (Just how much would a flight to Denver cost for three people *the day of!?*) Now I was worried about my youngest daughter crying in the backseat. (Pretty sure she thought this dramatic scene would end in divorce!) And I was almost certain I had pushed my husband over the edge.

So I sat up straight, composed myself as best I could, and attempted to persuade him that I really and truly would not act like a basket case the entire way to Colorado. He glanced at me, gave me half a smile, and kept driving back to Austin. I used all the logic I could to get him to stop and turn around, but nothing could touch his resolve.

When he pulled in the driveway, I knew there was no turning him around. It was done. And we all headed inside to talk it out. I have to tell you, he was masterful. He never got angry—never shamed or scorned. As a matter of fact, just the opposite. We all sat down in the family room and he prayed with us. Afterward, he gave us quick hugs and got back on the road while we called the airline to schedule a flight. It all worked out beautifully in the end. (Miraculously, the flights weren't too outrageous.) But mainly, Superman made his man-move and saved the day—thereby saving the vacation—and even more critical, the relationship. Mission accomplished.

That whole situation reminded me of something I often forget in the day-in, day-out of daily living. Boys will be boys—and my husband is still one of them.

Boys Will Be Boys

While there are many derogatory references associated with the phrase "boys will be boys," I want to assert that the statement is actually positive. News to you? Then I think it's important to understand some of how and why we have the wrong idea.

Lately, it's become pretty hip to dilute the traditional roles between men and women. In the past fifty years, we've been a part of a shift in thinking about how a man and a woman fit in a traditional family. Why, just look at how your grandmother fulfilled her familial role, compared to your mom, compared to you. We've come a long way, baby.

Loads of cultural shifts and political agendas and practical necessities brought the changes. And many influential writers chronicled the changes impacting the stereotypical roles fulfilled by men and women, but none tapped into the mental and emotional malaise of women nationwide more powerfully than Betty Friedan. In the late seventies, Friedan penned *The Feminine Mystique*. And in it, she espoused that it was the mystique of "feminine fulfillment" (defined as being married, having kids, and staying home) that doomed many women. As a matter of fact, she implied that women (and in particular housewives) themselves were actually displaced in American society—"virtual schizophrenics"—compelled to fill a role that left them largely unhappy and ridiculously underutilized.

Through her writings, she espoused that a woman fulfilling a traditionally feminine role—that of wife, mom, and home keeper—was missing the boat. She tapped the nerve of any woman who understands what it feels like to spend all day changing dirty diapers, re-wiping countertops sticky with apple juice, and trying in vain to catch a chance to read the daily news. In her book, she points out the plight of the American housewife:

> In the fifteen years after World War II, this mystique of feminine fulfillment became the cherished and self-perpetuating core of contemporary American culture. Millions of women lived their lives in the image of those pretty pictures of the American suburban housewife, kissing their husbands good-bye in front of the picture window, depositing their stationwagonsful of children at school, and smiling as they ran the new electric waxer over the spotless kitchen floor. They baked their own bread, sewed their own and their children's clothes, kept their new washing machines and dryers running all day. They changed the sheets on the beds twice a week instead of once, took the rug-hooking class in adult education, and pitied their poor frustrated mothers, who had dreamed of having a career. Their only dream was to be perfect wives and mothers; their highest ambition to have five children and a beautiful house; their only fight to get and keep their husbands. They had no thought for the unfeminine problems of the world outside the home; they wanted the men to make the major decisions. They gloried in their role as women, and wrote proudly on the census blank: "Occupation: housewife."[1]

In a sixty-thousand-word manuscript, Friedan not only gave frustrated housewives permission to revolt, but she managed to degrade those who considered themselves housewives. She sparked a revolution, eventually extinguishing the term altogether (who dares to call herself a housewife?) and diminishing the credibility of a role that is distinctly feminine.

The "Outmoded Masculine Mystique"

Now before you write me off as a Friedan hater, I need to confess that I appreciate her writings. She pushed the boundaries on traditional thinking and opened the doors for women in ways that are too numerous to mention in this chapter. But in any revolution—even one with words—there are casualties. And it seems even Friedan realized that men (and traditional male roles) ended up the object of some serious anger. Some years after the release of *The Feminine Mystique*, she was quoted as saying, "Men weren't really the enemy—they were fellow victims suffering from an outmoded masculine mystique that made them feel unnecessarily inadequate when there were no bears to kill."[2]

"An outmoded masculine mystique" is certainly an enlightening concept. And I think Friedan was right on in unearthing the truth about it. While women in the sixties and seventies were grasping for some much-needed liberation, men were struggling to find a new place to plant their feet. And while many women were exerting independence, many men were in turn tamed by this "new concept." It was this—the angst at large in culture—that created confusion. For men who were comfortable with the stereotypical roles of breadwinner and family leader, Friedan was dead on when she said that men felt "inadequate when there were no bears to kill."

For men, that time marked the start of a period of uncertainty about their role in the lives of women. Even little things like opening the door for women became a debate. Was it polite or offensive? Supportive or demeaning? And as those questions lurked around unanswered, men have struggled to find a voice on what it means to be positive and positively masculine.

Author John Eldredge has found a voice with men attempting to find those bears. In his book *Wild at Heart*, he seeks to unravel the lost male mystique, those inner secrets of a man's soul. He writes:

A Battle to fight. An Adventure to live. A Beauty to rescue. This is what a man longs for. This is what makes him come alive. Look at the films men love. For that matter, look at the dreams of little boys, the games they play. There is something fierce, passionate, and wild in the heart of every man. That is how he bears the image of God. And the reason that most men "live lives of quiet desperation" (Thoreau) is because men have been told that the reason God put them on earth is to be a good boy. To be nice.

God designed men to be dangerous. Simply look at the dreams and desires written in the heart of every boy: To be a hero, to be a warrior, to live a life of adventure and risk. Sadly, most men abandon those dreams and desires—aided by a Christianity that feels like nothing more than pressure to be a nice guy. It is no wonder that many men avoid church, and those who go are often passive and bored to death.

Now, in all your boyhood dreams growing up, did you ever dream of becoming a nice guy? Ladies, was the Prince of your dreams dashing . . . or merely nice? "We've taken away the dreams of a man's heart and told him to play the man." As C. S. Lewis said, "We castrate the gelding and bid him be fruitful."[3]

Wow. For me, it's the C. S. Lewis quote that hits the hardest. The irony of it—and the truth of it in my own life. Because how many times have I unintentionally attempted to warp my husband's masculinity by mandating safety, passivity, and rule keeping? How many times have I squelched his dream? Asked him to put down the metaphorical weapons of battle? How many times have I asked him to be nice and not so dangerous? How many times have I failed to let my man be one of the boys?

Let Boys Be Boys

What you may not realize is that as a woman, you have a tremendous amount of power over the man you're married to. In many ways, you hold the key to avoiding what Lewis calls "the castration." In millions of little ways, you can either affirm your husband's masculinity or you can crush it. I truly believe if wives really understood the depth of power they possess purely by passion, proximity, and physicality, they would feel secure in understanding their worth and value as women. If we could just grasp the fundamental issue of how relationship and marriage impact a man, we would stand tall and marvel in amazement, wielding our influence for positive change.

Author Rick Johnson knows the power of a wife's affirmation. In his book *The Man Whisperer*, he explains: "A woman has incredible power. She can destroy her man with her words or she can help him become the man he could never be without her support, faith, and encouragement. There's not much a man can't deal with in life if he knows he can come home to a loving, supportive wife who respects him."[4]

It's the encouragement part that interests me. And hopefully

Society at large can't make up its mind about men. Having spent the last thirty years redefining masculinity into something more sensitive, safe, manageable and, well, feminine, it now berates men for not being men. Boys will be boys, they sigh. As though if a man were to truly grow up he would forsake wilderness and wanderlust and settle down, be at home forever in Aunt Polly's parlor. "Where are all the real men?" is regular fare for talk shows and new books. You asked them to be women, *I wanted to say. The result is a gender confusion never experienced at such a wide level in the history of the world. How can a man know he is one when his highest aim is minding his manners?*[5]

John Eldredge

that gets you going as well. Because the truth be told, a man is not going to find better encouragement and inspiration anywhere on earth than from his wife. Not from his job or his salary. Not from athletic achievement or professional status. Plain and simple, it's meant to come from you, his wife, esteeming and respecting who God designed him to be as a man. That's truly the key to not only maxing out your marriage relationship, but it's also the key to promoting your husband to the man he's meant to be.

> Women are the reason we get up every day. I'm talking about real men. I wake up every day for a woman—to make it happen for her.[6]
>
> Steve Harvey

Let the Tinkering Begin

If you don't already know, men like tinkering. Under the hood of a car, on a boat, in the backyard, or in the garage. From their earliest days, guys are engaged in understanding *how things work* in order to *make them work*. So truly, one of the easiest ways to let your husband man up is by simply allowing him to fix things.

It's exactly what Will did in his Superman moment described at the beginning of the chapter. When we got in the car to go to Colorado, he was immediately presented with a problem. So he decided to fix it. I can just imagine his thought pattern that early June morning: *Susie has lost it. Susie is freaking out. She has major baggage from her wreck. Hmmm. We're at mile 25 of a thousand-mile trip. I can't talk her down. She won't settle down. It's time to turn around.* And with that (no discussion required), he turned the car around. That's how men work.

Men don't like to be presented with a problem to *discuss it*; they like to think they're presented with a problem to *fix it*. For many wives, it would go a long way to get this one through your head—men like to fix things. Therefore, if you need to have a lengthy discussion and sort out your feelings, well, talk to your girlfriend. However, if you have something that needs doing or fixing, take it to your man.

The Danger Zone

Another area in which wives would be well served with a reminder is this: men are wired to enjoy adventure and adventure is rarely safe. I honestly think that the reason Jack Bauer 24-type programs are so big is because men are adventure hungry. They are so emasculated by culture and necessity of a 24/7 desk job that their lack of expression is somehow mildly satiated by watching actors engage in it.

Men have an innate desire to express masculinity through bodily force—and your husband is no exception. Though you might think he fits the mild-mannered Clark Kent persona, working nine to five, there is a Superman hidden somewhere beneath. It might leak out clearing the back forty of trees with a chain saw or moving hay bales. It could be manifested by cycling seventy miles or running a marathon. For many, it's extreme-type sports. But whatever it is, most women feel as if it's a little unnecessary and more than slightly over the edge.

For my husband, it means cycling even after being hit by a car. For one friend's husband, it means continuing to water-ski after multiple surgeries and numerous visits to the emergency room. For my seventy-three-year-old dad, it means playing a rough-and-tumble game of handball three to four times a week. For my brother-in-law, it means singlehandedly building a deck that hangs over a cliff. These men are merely reflecting what's naturally inside of them—a desire to express and embrace the physicality of their masculine nature regardless of the exertion and danger.

As wives, we must let them.

Be the "Yes" in His Life

The final biggie in promoting your husband and letting him man up is achieved when you are the "yes" in his life. Most men have big dreams—they tend to be visionaries. When we as wives focus too inwardly, we can unintentionally squelch those big dreams. We can be a little too safe, a little too cautious, and, well, just a little too little in our thinking. As wives, it's our job to be the yes in their lives, not the no. And that means even when their dreams are big or scary.

I would say that the biggest, scariest dream Will proposed to me was leaving our secure, nice-paying job at an established denominational church in Fort Worth to start a new, nondenominational church in Austin. We had no insurance (with two kids and one on the way), no assurance of income, and no future security. Nada. It was a big dream with more unknowns than I could count. Many people advised against it, but somehow I had the confidence to say yes. And in all honesty, I was about the only yes in Will's life at that time. Most of the people around, while entranced with the idea, were willing to be bystanders but not participants in the dream. It was just a little too edgy and a little too wild.

But fifteen years later, that dream of his supports thirty-five staff members and an annual budget of 5.5 million dollars. It has changed countless lives and continues to impact not only Austin, but lives around the world through global missions. It was a dream worth the risk but one that would have died had I said no. Without my support, Will would not have been willing to take the risk. Without my support, the church would not be here today. I didn't realize until years later what my yes meant for Will's life, my life, and the lives of thousands of others who have been touched by Austin Christian Fellowship.

It's part of our calling as wives to be the yes, not the no. That is the yes our men need to have the confidence to see the challenge and surmount it.

When Harvey Mansfield, a seventy-four-year-old professor at Harvard University and author of *Manliness*, was asked to define *manliness*, he said, "My quick definition is 'confidence with risk.'"[7] And I couldn't agree more. Men desire the adventure to take the hill and to rise in victory. But the amazing thing about marriage is that we, as wives, can actually be the confidence our husbands need. When they see the risk, it is our yes that becomes their confidence. And that yes is more powerful than any inborn belief they have about their own ability. I believe that a wife has the capacity to be a man's greatest assurance of all—simply by being his yes.

> *I've noticed that so often our word to boys is don't. Don't climb on that, don't break anything, don't be so aggressive, don't be so noisy, don't be so messy, don't take such crazy risks. But God's design—which he placed in boys as the picture of himself—is a resounding yes. Be fierce, be wild, be passionate.*[8]
>
> John Eldredge

It's true that boys will be boys—and that's a good thing!

Uncovering the Truth

- *Looking back at your personal history, think about the transition in traditional roles in your extended family. How different is your role as wife and mother from your mother's or your grandmother's? What are some of the positive changes? How about the negative ones?*

- *What do you see as the biggest stumbling block in allowing your husband to man up?*

- *When your husband tries to tinker and fix things, what is your first reaction?*

- *Does your husband have a dangerous tendency? What is it? How could you respond to it in a positive way and allow him to express his masculinity?*

- *When have you been a yes in your husband's life? A no?*

THE MALE ROOM:
Responses from Real Men Who Love Their Wives

In your opinion, what makes a "real man"?

DAVE: The ability to grill, a love for John Wayne and the Three Stooges, and the ability to control his bodily noises until the most opportune moment. Okay, for real. A man who recognizes his own shortcomings and allows the people he cares about to fill in his areas of weakness. A man who is comfortable enough with himself to love deeply and openly. A man who recognizes his unique God-created man-qualities and allows God to work through them.

SAM: A real man loves God more than anyone else, puts God first in everything. He loves God more than his wife and kids. A real man makes decisions based on God's Word and promises no matter how painful it is, no matter how unpopular it is, no matter how uncomfortable it is. A real man tells the truth all the time. A real man doesn't succumb to the pressures of the world.

BARRY: A real man is someone who is authentic about his weaknesses, eager to become more like Christ, and committed to loving his family and others as a result of his being loved by God. Real men are willing to live in both toughness and tenderness, depending upon the circumstances and needs of oneself and others. [Footnote 1: They can also watch at least three games at once through the use of the DVR, remote, and/or multiple televisions. Footnote 2: They would also blow a squirrel out of their backyard tree with a .357 Magnum and not even blink or experience one pang of guilt.]

What is the one thing that you wish your wife really understood about being a man?

DAVE: That we truly are as clueless about many things as we seem. Many of the aspects of life women hold most dear are meaningless to us. We will do our best to act like we care, but we will never care as much as you do. Just as you do not care about the nickel package defense in football.

SAM: Does it have to be one? This could be an entire book! I wish she understood the pressure we face. There's so much pressure coming at us from every angle. Pressure to perform, pressure to provide, pressure to be a better husband, pressure to be a better dad. Pressure to be perfect. I wish she understood that we are under constant attack and that we can never let our guard down. I wish she understood how much sex means to a man. OK, I'll stop there! Got that off my chest.

BARRY: I wish she better understood the very real tension between appropriate, healthy sexuality and common, everyday temptations, even lust, that men face. I know that men and women are wired differently when it comes to all that, but it *seems* as though she doesn't sense the power and pull of temptation on me, especially in the visual sense. The reality is accepted, but not the intensity.

Men like risks. What is the one risk you'd love to take if only you had your wife's blessing?

DAVE: I don't see them as risks as much as see them as tests. Can I actually jump over the lawn chair and through the inner tube into the pool without breaking some part of my body? It's a test of my athleticism. Would I have the courage to actually jump out of a plane with only a parachute to save my life? It's a test, not a risk. I'm very lucky. My wife doesn't really stop me from trying a test I truly want to take. She does, however, point out the relative risk of failing the test. That sometimes deters me from my quest. The only thing I think she keeps me from testing is my physical abilities. As I have aged, she has become quite protective of me and doesn't want me to hurt myself physically. I still feel the need to test my strength and athletic prowess on occasion. As usual, she is probably right.

BARRY: To climb the Matterhorn or some other especially dangerous peak provided I could still even do it.

SAM: To be a missionary.

4

Get Over Your Naked Self

YOU WON'T LOVE SHARING WHAT YOU LOATHE

If you got 66,000 text messages a day, you'd be pretty over-whelmed, right? I mean, who in the world could have that much to say to you? But what if I told you that of those 66,000, some 46,200 were negative, mean-spirited texts? On top of that, let's say that they were all from the same person. Not only would you be angry and offended, but you'd probably realize that the sender didn't have your best interest at heart to say the very least! You'd probably think they were crazy.

Weird scenario, but pertinent to real life, because the truth is, you send about 66,000 messages to yourself every day. Obviously I'm not talking about texts—it's actually called *self-talk*. Psychologists tell us that on the average, you and I send 66,000 internal messages daily. And the startling thing is that about 70 percent of those messages are negative. That's a heck of a lot of self smack-talk.

Think about it: You wake up first thing in the morning, look in the mirror, and say, "Gosh, I look horrible." You step on the scale and say, "Oh great. I've gained another pound." That's negative self-talk, which is not only counterproductive, it's a little bit crazy. It means you are bombarding yourself every single day with horrible, devastating internal texts. It happens so quickly and so often that sometimes it can take you by surprise. Like just yesterday.

I was waiting in line at my local grocery store, standing there in jeans, a T-shirt, and my favorite flip-flops, and I glanced over and saw Faith Hill on the cover of *Shape* magazine. Now, I love Faith Hill—her music is great and I think she's wonderful—but when I looked at her posing on the cover in a yellow bikini all airbrushed and beautiful, I felt like puking. Apparently, Faith decided that this year on her birthday (instead of a Benz or a trip to Paris with her yum husband, Tim McGraw) she would gift herself with a cover shoot in an itsy-bitsy floral bikini. She was quoted as saying, "Wearing a bikini on a magazine cover is my 41st birthday present to myself."[1] All I could think as I stood staring, transfixed on her forty-one-year-old perfection was, *Gee, what a great idea. I wish I had thought of that. . . .* And then I had a flood of more sarcastic thoughts about what I would look like, should I land on the cover of a magazine. The headlines weren't pretty.

It all happened so fast. I was just standing there minding my own business, waiting in line. I innocently glanced to the left to scan the headlines, then *boom*—before I realized it, I was assaulted with hate mail in my mind. *Wow . . . she looks amazing at forty-one. Hmmm. Good gracious, her abs . . . is that a six pack? Her boobs look so perfect—maybe plastic? Hopefully plastic. Tiny bathing suit. I wore one like that in high school, but I*

> *Are you waiting to be skinnier, thinner, more toned, more tanned, better dressed, sexier, more lovable, nicer, smarter, funnier, or wealthier before you really begin your life? Millions of us are. And it's a complete waste of time. Body obsession and the quest for perfection are destroying our lives, and we are willing partners in this destruction.*[2]
>
> Jessica Weiner

don't think I ever looked that good. Certainly not now. Nope. That's not anywhere near me. Humph—I certainly won't be peeling down to my skivvies anytime soon. Nowhere near soon.

In a matter of a few minutes, I went from pretty much liking what was going on with my body to really feeling bad about me. From loving to loathing in zero to sixty.

Haters and Comparers

As I finished up at the checkout line and carried my groceries out, my heart was stabbed with a piercing truth. It might as well have burst from the blue Texas sky like a fireball. This is what I heard: "You know what, Susie? It's incredibly hard to love yourself when you are comparing yourself to Faith. Quit comparing and stop hating. Delete that text. You can't love what you loathe."

See, the problem in comparison (especially when it's me versus Faith Hill) is that we end up silently berating ourselves and opening the floodgate of negative self-talk. And negative self-talk isn't healthy for your body or your mind—or your relationships.

I would even venture to say that comparing ourselves to the perfection we see on billboards, television, the big screen, and magazine covers is the number one thing that brings women down. It generates an ongoing tape of negative self-talk in our heads, and we end up labeling ourselves with statements like: "I'm fat." "I'm ugly." "My face is wrinkled." "My boobs are too small." "My butt is too big." The text goes on and on—over and over—and at the end of the day there sits a woman who hates what she sees. And she hates it so much that she is reluctant to share it with the man she loves. It's just not possible to present your whole self to a man if you hate the self you're presenting. That kind of negative body image has the potential to wreck your sex life, putting a sizable dent in your marriage relationship.

So where's the how-to on loving what you've got—and embracing the inevitable nakedness in your marriage with confidence and joy?

Ditch the Hope for a Plastic Pact

For the last couple years, I mused aloud that if only all women (or at least my closest friends) would make a pact not to do the plastic surgery thing, that would make everybody more okay. As I reached my forties, I found more and more friends looking just a little tighter and a little lighter in oh-so-subtle ways. I noticed a mysterious rounded lift in the breasts or a thinning of the once-paunchy baby tummy. There was suddenly an absence of smile lines and squinty eyes. And of course, a slightly puffed, inexpressive forehead. It made me rather desperate—feeling the need to encourage everyone I knew to pledge to the no-plastic pact. But then something very funny happened.

Over the course of a month, I ran across several articles about the rise of plastic surgery among women and the resulting effect on men. They all said about the same thing, but it was the article by Tom Chiarella that really was poignant. His piece is entitled "How Men Really Feel about Breast Implants." He writes:

Encountering an augmented breast for the first time is a bit like sitting in a very expensive car before a test drive. It's unfamiliar and more than a little exciting. It's different from your normal ride. Things have been tricked up. It may be bigger than you're used to, and certain places are firmer, appear

60

newer, seem to offer a different kind of function. You can't help responding to the features—the DVD player in the console, the fancy steering wheel, the huge speakers. You shake your head; it is, after all a car. Still, you feel lured.

But when you get intimate with the augmented breast, two things are certain: You can always feel the implant, and the feeling will always lead you to the conscious realization that someone pimped this breast. . . . The truth is in the touch.[4]

Chiarella's reference to the pimped breast made me laugh out loud, but there was something else that caught my attention and cleared my mind on this whole issue of the drive and need for a perfect body presentation. And it is this: my body, where Will is concerned, is not just something to be looked at—it was meant to be touched. While culture might focus on the appeal and look of airbrushed plastic perfection, in marriage the emphasis is on the real deal: authentic naked physical intimacy.

As a woman, embracing your body is as important to your marriage as almost anything. Because while physical love may have many different kinds of manifestations, like a hug or a gentle pat on the back, sex is an exclusive kind of touching. And it's the one act meant to be shared with your husband alone.

Be Sexy in Your Own Skin

Now you might be thinking, *Okay, I get the whole touch thing, but it's hard to feel energized about getting stripped down and touched when you've got some "problem areas." You know, cellulite, sagging boobs, stretch marks, etc.* And maybe you have been trying to tackle toning up and losing twenty pounds for the last decade or so. It's a common dilemma, and you might be tempted to keep it all in the dark, but I say, don't let the imperfections control you. Because it's really not all about how you look (I know that this might be a hard pill to swallow); instead, it's much more about an attitude. Most men would agree that a woman is most attractive when she feels attractive and acts attractive. When she is able to exude a confidence in her own sensuality. That kind of confidence is often lost on even the most beautiful of women, which to me is entirely sad.

Girlfriends, sexy starts as a frame of mind. It's born from knowing you're appealing. And in this case, not to the masses, but to the one man who matters most: your husband. And the fact of the matter is, once your man is touching you—should he be a good man who is full of the best kind of love—he ceases to focus on how you look and begins to think of the pleasure of making you feel good. And when that is going on, it should make you feel immensely sexy in the one and only place sexy belongs: marriage.

> In reading all the letters from men, I was struck by their depth of sensitivity about the issue of women's appearance. It wasn't an impersonal, animal reaction (as it is with women the men don't personally know), it was a deeply personal one. The wife's comfort with and appreciation of her own body and femininity, and her willingness to share that with her husband, actually fed his sense of well-being, his feeling of being loved as a husband and as a "man."[5]
>
> Dr. Laura Schlessinger

So how do you get to that place of appreciating, loving, and actually being comfortable with the body that you've got? Of being able to be sexy in your own skin with your husband? You want to hear something that might just sound amazingly absurd? I think it all starts in your spirit. As crazy as this might seem, I truly believe it all starts with God.

From the Inside Out

See, God wants you to love yourself—wholly and deeply. He wants you to be able to love yourself—body included—with an unconditional love. That's exactly the way that he loves you. He made you (Gen. 1:27). And you are marvelously made (Ps. 139:14). As a matter of fact, God himself regards you as the crowning work of all creation, the best thing he ever created (Ps. 8:5–8). He doesn't want you to hate on yourself and then extend that self-loathing and its effects into your relationships. In the New Testament, there's a verse about this very principle. Jesus is confronted by some theologians who ask him to tell them which of the Ten Commandments is the greatest one of all. And Jesus—I imagine without hesitation—said this: "'Love the Lord your God with all your heart and with all your soul and with all your mind.' This is the first and greatest commandment. And the second is like it: 'Love your neighbor as yourself'" (Matt. 22:35–39).

Jesus in effect was saying, "Hey, love God. With all that is in you, love him. And remember to love your neighbor too. And you know what—be sure and love yourself." That's definitely a Susie paraphrase, but think it through on a personal level. When you love God, you don't smack talk him, right? And certainly, if you truly love your neighbor, you wouldn't talk negatively about them. Well, then, the same is true for you too. If you love yourself, you should keep from letting all that negative self-talk roll around in your head. It's just not fitting to say hateful things about someone you love. And while we all understand that and probably think it's a smart idea, in practice it can get a little difficult.

I was confronted with that difficulty in the grocery store when I saw the magazine cover. And to keep from surrendering to the smack dialogue, I had to go through a little exercise to disengage from comparing myself to the Faith Hill photo so that I wouldn't start hating on myself.

Right as I pulled out of the grocery store parking lot, I had to remind myself that Faith Hill is a celebrity who has been gifted with a lovely and *extraordinary* life. One laden with a staff of people who help her look completely amazing all of the time. To get her body (and face) looking like that at forty-one means that she has the time, money, and energy to devote to some serious luxuriating. She likely has a team of people assigned to help her pretty her face and teeth, motivate her to work on those amazing abs, and babysit the kids while she gets it all done. Those are privileges not often found in an ordinary woman's life. Someone like you and me—with a more ordinary body, an ordinary face, and an ordinary income.

We have to get over always holding up an extraordinary example as the norm where physical beauty is concerned. And we must stop comparing ourselves, because the comparison leads to hating, and the hating leads to problems being naked—both in the head and in the bed.

Fit and Lucky

Now I have spent some time here building a case for culture as the big bad wolf of self-esteem in women—of robbing regular women of the ability to feel attractive sexually. And I have also spent some time underlining how incredibly important it is to be able to love yourself the way God loves you. But there is another problem that seems ever present in the lives of women everywhere that keeps them locked in to a hater mentality with their own bodies.

American women, and especially moms, are notorious for taking care of everyone else but themselves. I have many mom friends who work their fingers to the bone, at the expense of their own health, to provide financially for their kids to do all sorts of amazing things like elite soccer or after-school tutoring. We can't find the time to work out or eat right because we're too tired and too stressed out. And the thought of adding *one more thing* to our already stuffed list of things to do is just maddening. So we don't. We take care of the kids, managing their overbooked lives, and we attempt to take care of the house (though from the looks of it, it's hard to tell), but we flat-out won't make time to care for our bodies. And the neglect is evident every time we look in the mirror—and that makes us feel bad. Real bad. Then the negative mojo floods every part of our being, infecting our self-esteem and our sexuality.

If this is you, you know it. And it stings. If you eat like a teenager, scarfing whatever comes your way without regard to the impact, you feel it sitting on your hips. If you can't remember the last time you did some type of cardio something, the truth of it haunts you. The thing is, we know better. We really do. There are numerous studies to prove that when we take care of ourselves, we feel better about ourselves. No matter our age or stage in life, getting healthy makes for a healthy self-esteem. And that translates into our marital relationships in more ways than one.

We know the way out—start eating healthier and moving more—but for some reason, it doesn't do much to motivate. Those commonsense things that we know we should be doing remain undone. And when they are undone, our self-esteem comes undone.

So, I've come up with a novel new plan: If just getting out there and getting it done doesn't move you, how about a move to Paris? Yep. Move to Paris, France. Kind of a big step for such a small problem as eating right and exercising, but it might just help. See, what you might not know is, not only are Parisian women fit, not fat, but they seem to enjoy a healthy sex life too. Pamela Druckerman of the *Washington Post* explains:

> If I have to get old, I want to do it in Paris.
>
> It's not because of the dank weather, the constant personal snubs or a fetish for unpasteurized cheese. It's because, quite frankly, I'd like to keep having sex.
>
> In the United States, my odds would be grim. Through our 40s, we American women manage to arrange romps on a fairly regular basis. But the latest national statistics show that by our 50s, a third of us haven't had sex in the last year. By our 60s, nearly half have gone sexless in the previous year. Once

we hit our 70s, most of us might as well hang up an "out of business" sign. (Needless to say, men fare much better.)

So much for the gym-bodied baby boomers who promised to make 60 the new 40, using Botox as an aphrodisiac. Among today's 50-plus women, the problem of sexlessness is as bad or worse than it was for older women two decades ago.

But not in France. Frenchwomen simply don't suffer from the same dramatic, post-40s slide into sexual obsolescence. Just 15 percent of Frenchwomen in their 50s and 27 percent in their 60s haven't had any sex in the past year, according to a 2004 national survey by France's Regional Health Observatory. Another national survey being released next month will report that cohabiting Frenchwomen over 50 are having more sex now than they did in the early 1990s.

Try not to hate them: Frenchwomen don't get fat, and they do get lucky.[6]

Now, I'm obviously being sarcastic about fixing a problem like working out and eating right by moving to France, but I do think the article is of interest. And I think there is something to learn here from our feisty French sisters. They're not letting the downward momentum get them down. Druckerman further explains, "Older women in Paris don't actually look any better than the ones in New York. The difference is that the French typically don't see sex as a privilege for the young and beautiful. They see it as one of life's most basic pleasures—something women or men would not give up without a fight."[7]

So, ladies, let's just boil it down here: we need to work out and eat right. And we need to delete all those negative texts as quickly as they pop up. To truly love, we've got to embrace a God concept of how we're made, because it's then that we'll start getting comfortable inside our own sexy skin. And finally, I say we should all learn a little lesson from those French women—because sex isn't just a privilege for the perfect. As a matter of fact, in marriage, it's one of the finest pleasures of all.

We've just got to stop the personal loathing and start loving instead. Because I don't know about you, but I think sexless at sixty sounds kind of scary.

Uncovering the Truth

- *Be honest here: can you say that you love yourself—including your body? If God could talk to you directly, what might he want to say to you about this?*

- *What do you do when you experience negative "texting"?*

- *List three tools you have on hand to extinguish the lies and fan the flames of truth when negative messages surface.*

- *How has a negative self-image impacted your ability to get naked with your husband? What are some practical ways you can change things and embrace your sexuality—for yourself and your marriage?*

THE MALE ROOM:
Responses from Real Men Who Love Their Wives

Would you rather look at or touch your wife's body?

BEN: Yes. It's like Braille. You kind of want to read with your hands.

MICHAEL: Touch.

BARRY: Obviously, men are largely visual, so looking for me has always been enjoyable for a large part of our marriage. And it still is to some degree, but age, babies, surgeries, time, etc., also negatively impact the attractiveness of a woman's body. And we men have to accept and be understanding that some of those changes she cannot help or control. On the other hand, our personal worlds and the world around us, including the "Christian" world, are still filled with women who are naturally very attractive or who even try to be "extra" attractive to men. To me that argues that women still need to be willing to do what they can to remain appropriately attractive, even "seductive" toward their husbands with their bodies. I want that attractiveness from my wife physically, but that's never been a high priority to her. And when I talk about it, it's usually not a very enjoyable or productive discussion. Therefore, my greater enjoyment comes from touching at this stage of our lives, and thankfully she is a beautiful person in many other ways.

How do you think the way your wife feels about her body impacts your sexual relationship?

BARRY: I've tried to not allow it to be a major deterrent, but in the big scheme of things it does decrease how compelling she is physically.

MICHAEL: I think it can inhibit intimacy because she can be too self-conscious about aspects that are not really important to me.

BEN: When my wife thinks she looks good, she feels and acts sexier—no doubt about it. But if she thinks she's unattractive, then she's less likely to want to share herself with me.

If you could be completely honest with your wife about her body, what would you say to her?

BARRY: "I wish you would just try to make your body more of a priority. You don't need to be a supermodel, become an aerobics instructor, or look like anyone else. But when you don't try, it's at best disappointing and does take away from what we might enjoy more if things were different. It's a little bit like if I didn't try to get better at communicating with you. While we still might communicate you would be sad because you knew there was the possibility for more."

MICHAEL: "You are perfect just the way you are."

BEN: I would tell her that she is fearfully and wonderfully made by God. I'd tell her that she is a gift to me and that it is a gift to my life to be able to engage physically/sexually with her.

5

Are You Laughing or Crying?

HOW A HAPPY HEART MAKES A HAPPY MARRIAGE

I work in a very dangerous job environment. It's not a *Man vs. Wild* situation, but it is dangerous nonetheless. You see, I work with a man who makes me laugh. And what's equally precarious, I make him laugh too.

Now, you might be wondering how in the world that could be a dangerous situation. You might even be thinking that sounds like a great work environment. And I must admit it is, but just imagine this scenario: I wake up early every weekday morning. I get dressed and gather my stuff for the day while my weary husband snoozes away. Then, just before I scoot out the door to my on-air radio job, I give Will a little peck on the cheek and I'm gone.

After a fifteen-minute commute, I stroll into the studio where my morning cohosts, Gary and Roxanne, have been engaging the listeners for the previous hour. Within minutes, I pop on my headphones, and my quiet morning turns into on-air improv. We make up the *Family Friendly Morning* team on Austin's 102.3 The River, and it's our job to entertain the listeners. The deal is that much of that entertainment is born in the dialogue between Gary and me because we just happen to look at life from polar extremes. He is the caustic, sarcastic, quintessential man who pokes fun at me at every opportunity. I am, on the other hand, the sunny, optimistic, quintessential woman. And I can't exactly tell you why, but the verbal sparring between us makes the sparks fly. It's funny—genuinely funny. And though we play certain on-air roles, the fact is that we routinely make each other laugh. Not only that, but Gary has Roxanne in stitches too. It's comedy central for hours on end with that man. Sometimes the morning shows with Gary and Roxanne are so funny, I laugh my mascara right off.

So how in the world could I call my work environment dangerous when it's so fun? What kind of trouble could a woman and a man get into if they're routinely laughing hysterically at one another?

Well, that's something to think about. Now, you likely have heard or know firsthand that women typically like and seek out a man with a "good sense of humor"—that's common sense. But what you may not know is that women laugh 126 percent more than men, and that factor ends up being a critical component in the relationship.[1] A woman's laughter quotient is so vital that it can actually be used to measure attraction. Check out the stats here:

> In 3,745 ads placed on April 28, 1996, in eight papers from the *Baltimore Sun* to the *San Diego Union-Tribune*, females were 62% more likely to mention laughter in their ads, and women were more likely to seek out a "sense of humor" while men were more likely to offer it. Clearly, women seek men who make them laugh, and men are eager to comply with this request. When Karl Grammar and Irenaus Eibl-Eibesfeldt studied spontaneous conversations between mixed-sex pairs of young German adults meeting for the first time, they noted that the more a woman laughed aloud during these encoun-

ters, the greater her self-reported interest in the man she was talking to.[2]

It doesn't take a relational genius or a German study to say that when a woman laughs at a man's jokes, it's a form of flattery. Both sexes instinctively know this—it's typically a huge part of flirting. When a woman laughs at a man's jokes, she is telling him he's funny, smart, and yes, even attractive. Laughter energizes the relationship and the attraction.

Senior Coffee Anyone?

Aside from acting as a tool for measuring attraction, laughter has loads of other benefits. Psychologist and laughter therapist (not joking here) Steve Wilson says, "The effects of laughter and exercise are very similar."[3] Laughing increases your blood flow, increases infection-fighting antibodies, and stabilizes blood sugar—just like exercise. All good. But besides that, it has other important perks. U.S. Army Reserve Colonel James Scott, who works at the Pentagon serving family members of those in the National Guard, says, "Laughter is an important stress-management tool. When you laugh, the brain stops thinking. It's a proven way to keep your mental balance."[4] The fact that laughter provides stress relief—and creates a pause in brain function—makes it one of the key reasons that laughter is such an important ingredient in your marriage.

Will and I laugh a lot. Our house is full of the stuff. Some of it is because I can be incredibly playful, and some of it is because Will is witty and smart. But I never fully understood the importance of laughter in our relationship or appreciated its role as a pause or reset button until last summer.

We got in a horrible argument. It was about money—and it was about sex. A double whammy and a real doozy. It was so bad that it lasted several days. A simmering fight—the kind that sits on the hotplate ready to blow at any minute. As a matter of fact, it was so bad that we had to leave the house to talk about it. I don't know if it was a subconscious, desperate attempt at entrapment—knowing if we left the house together, then we'd have to stay together and work it out. Or if we just knew that it was so ugly that it wasn't something we wanted our children to see. Whichever, we instinctively knew that we needed to leave to hash it apart and figure it out.

We decided on McDonald's. Sounds strange if you don't know us, but we're both helplessly addicted to Mickey D's coffee. And we also knew that our neighborhood McDonald's would be deserted at 3:30 on a Sunday afternoon. It was safe. And it would be quiet. We could talk openly, honestly, and pretend to be mature adults—something we hadn't done or been in days.

We walked heavily to the counter, and I placed my order: a small coffee with three creams on the side. Then Will went to order: a small black coffee. Just as he got the words out of his mouth, the cute young employee looked up at Will and said brightly, "Okay, one small coffee with cream and one senior coffee black."

I startled from my weary funk and stared at her. What she said was so absurd, I questioned her. "What did you just say?"

She looked at us confused and glanced at me, then back at Will. "A small coffee with cream for you, ma'am, and a senior coffee . . . for you, sir. Right?"

Will stood in shocked silence. Then he whispered to the cashier, "How old do you think I am?"

She stood bewildered, her eyes darting back and forth between me and Will.

When she repeated her question, I couldn't hold it in—she thought my fit forty-five-year-old husband was over sixty! I doubled over in laughter, convulsing so hard I was crying.

Will asked again, "How old do you think I am?"

"Ummm . . . well, I don't exactly know . . ." It was dawning on her that she had misjudged Will's age. "Um, I'm actually new and I don't really know how old you need to be to get a senior coffee . . . so . . ."

And then I burst out, "You have to be sixty years old! That's how old you have to be!" I put my head on the counter, laughing uncontrollably.

By this time, Will was laughing too—so tickled he could barely respond. "I'm just forty-five! I'm not that old. But since you asked, I'd definitely like that senior coffee now." Then with as much sarcasm as he could muster he said, "And pour her one too" as he pointed at me.

We waited, snickering and stealing sideward glances, while the embarrassed girl filled our coffees. When she finally brought us the tray, Will smiled at her kindly and told her it was no big deal. Then we stumbled from the counter, still laughing, and found a secluded booth. We sat down with every intent of discussing those heated matters that for days had driven us apart, but all we could do was look up and laugh at each other, sometimes loudly and sometimes just shaking our heads in disbelief. It was quite possibly the most enormously funny thing that had happened to us in years.

Ahhh . . .

What happened to us that afternoon in McDonald's is that humor redefined the situation. Will and I came in separated, ready to engage in battle with each other. We were both loaded with creative excuses for staying mad and making a point. The anger had isolated and detached us from one another. In a very real sense, we were using the anger to cop out of dealing with the problems. But what happened is that instantaneous humor was injected into our relationship. Like a sun shower, it popped up with lightning speed and drenched us both in the storm. We were completely defenseless—which also made it so completely effective. The laughter was infectious and cathartic. Just what our relationship needed most. And it's what helped us cope with the crisis.

The laughter provided a means of reducing the tension, and we were then able to discuss the real problems we had without all the emotional drama. It brought a cleansing perspective, and it gave us the energy we needed to sort out the problems in a more relaxed environment. It gave us the "ahhh" that we desperately needed.

Science supports the "ahhh" we felt. Hara Estroff Marano, of *Psychology Today*, reports that laughter may be just the thing couples need to keep their marriages together. She writes:

> Homegrown laughter may be what ailing couples need most. Uniquely human, laughter is, first and foremost, a social signal—it disappears when there is no audience, which may be as small as one other person—and it binds people together. It synchronizes the brains of speaker and listener so that they are emotionally attuned.
>
> These are the conclusions of Robert Provine, Ph.D., a neuroscientist who found that laughter is far too fragile to dissect in the laboratory. Instead, he observed thousands of incidents of laughter spontaneously occurring in everyday life, and wittily reports the results in *Laughter: A Scientific Investigation* (Penguin Books, 2001).
>
> Laughter establishes—or restores—a positive emotional climate and a sense of connection between two people, who literally take pleasure in the company of each other. For if there's one thing Dr. Provine found it's that speakers laugh even more than their listeners. Of course levity can defuse anger and anxiety, and in so doing it can pave the path to intimacy.
>
> Most of what makes people laugh is not thigh-slapper stuff but conversational comments. "Laughter is not primarily about humor," says Dr. Provine, "but about social relationships."[5]

What the article contends for couples is true: laughter paves the way to intimacy.

The Path to Intimacy

How many women do you know who have loads of laughter in their marriage relationships but are dragging around saying, "He just doesn't make me happy anymore"? None. There's a reason—laughing makes you feel good. Laughing sends those zippy, loving-life endorphins flooding through your brain, giving you a heightened sense of well-being personally and in your relationships.

If you are "just getting by" in your marriage, I would bet that you haven't laughed heartily in the past several months. Maybe you've allowed unforgiveness to linger, or perhaps you've let the pressure and stress of everyday life (or managing the kidlets) drain you dry. Don't let that happen! Play. Flirt. Listen to him. Laugh with him. And by all means, be willing to laugh at yourself. If you take yourself too seriously, you're likely to become a boring old married matron. That's not the woman he courted in the beginning. As a matter of fact, if you could view video footage of your early dating years, I'm betting that there would have been plenty of guffawing on your part. Plenty.

Getting in the Mood

The difficulty with getting in the mood—and embracing the whole laughing thing in your relationship—is that sometimes life cuts in on our best intentions. Like just yesterday. Here I am writing this chapter, feeling all happily married and everything, when there's a snafu.

Will and I had the ultimate happy weeknight. He came in from work while I was managing to get a healthy, tasty dinner on the table. We all actually sat down to eat at the dinner table like above-average Americans. About thirty minutes later, Will shuttled our fifteen-year-old Sara (the only kidlet left at home) off to her Bible study group. When he walked back in the door, he pointed out with flirty casualness that we had just enough time to take a tumble in "de boudoir" before one of our favorite programs started on TV. A perfect evening.

But the evening took a pointed, downward turn. About an hour later, Will went to pick up Sara, and when he returned, he crushed my "life couldn't get any better" mood. In abrupt manly style, Will burst through the door and said something incredibly thoughtless, and all my smiles and butterflies whooshed furiously out the window. When he realized what he had done, we talked it out. And though we pushed past personal defensiveness, I went to bed as wounded as ever.

I woke up the next morning stony cold. And the more I thought about the issue, the more unhappy I became. There was no laughing or smiling or "love my life" moments there at all. And the interesting thing was that Will was trying ever so gently to ease my mood with light humor. Pet names. Funny anecdotes. But I wouldn't bite. I was sullen and quiet. And I certainly didn't intend on laughing, thank you very much.

As the day progressed (or more accurately, digressed), everything Will did seemed to bother me. Why was he washing the car in the driveway when Sara was expecting friends in ten minutes? And as a matter of fact, why was he washing *his* car and not *my* car?! The list went on and on . . . and it wasn't until much later in the day I had a breakthrough. And it wasn't about Will cracking the perfect joke, nor was it the absurdity of a "senior coffee" moment. It came when I was on my way to a party with all my friends who ride horses at the same barn with me.

I was driving to the party, fuming and pouting, working up a teary tantrum all alone in the car. The just-right love song was playing on the radio, setting the tone for a super-duper pity party. And at my most desperate moment—the kind you get when your thoughts drag you off to, "He just doesn't make me happy"—I prayed a prayer, a true cry for help. It was not particularly eloquent. Rather, it was something like, "Dear God, help me. Help me." Not much more than that.

By the time I arrived at my friend Jennifer's house, I felt a simple calm wash over me. And I got out of the car, walked up to the door, and joined the ladies from my barn already inside enjoying a "horse warming" party. My equestrian buddy Jennifer had acquired a handsome horse and thought it a great opportunity to celebrate. There was fabulous food, wine, and talk of all things equine. Little did I know that a forlorn prayer and the girls' night out was just the thing I needed to unlock my unhappy heart.

The laughter that evening was nearly nonstop. From one story to the next, we hooted and snorted till our jaws hurt. By the time I dragged my laughter-worn body to the car, I was replete with "I love my life" endorphins. When I finally got home, Will was waiting up for me. And while I wanted to get defensive with him again (it was the first impulse I had), I resisted the urge and responded to his mildly funny greeting instead. I didn't laugh, but I smiled ever so warmly, beginning the meltdown of the tension between us.

A Spoonful of Sugar

What happened that night is a twofold power pack for finding your way back to loving your life—and more important, your spouse. First, I prayed. I recognized that I needed help beyond myself to get out of myself. I acknowledged that I had a problem and cried out in the right direction for help. Basically, I admitted I was too sick to fix my attitude. I asked God for help.

Second, I sought out friends. To be honest, I felt really tired on my way to that party. I easily could have let my funk wear me down and keep me home in my pajamas. But instead, I got myself dressed, drove to my friend's house, and joined the fun. And the deal is, those girls lifted my spirits. They didn't know they were doing it, but they were just the same. They gave me just the dose of laughter I needed to get out of my myopic state of mind and into a bigger, better place.

79

In Proverbs 17:22, there is an insightful little verse that says, "A cheerful heart is good medicine" (CEV). And in my case, I truly believe that my prayer was an admission of feeling sick—and I believe that my friends were the spoonful of sugar I needed to make the medicine of forgiveness go down.

I'm grateful for their laughter and their cheerful hearts. They helped me smile at Will when I got home. Because with that small gesture, I in essence said to him, "I love my life again. Everything is going to be okay. I forgive you, I love you, and I'm so happy I married you."

So, cry if you must and get it all out. And then . . . laugh.

Uncovering the Truth

- *Author Anna Fellows Johnston says, "Men need laughter sometimes more than food."[6] How much laughter does your husband need to stay full?*

- *Do you ever withhold smiles and laughter from your husband when you're mad? If you do, what exactly are you saying to him? Be detailed.*

- *Think about a time when laughter burst through a heated moment. What was the key ingredient in your attitude that allowed the breakthrough?*

- *If you are lacking laughter in your marriage, could that be a sign that there's some deep problem you've yet to acknowledge? What is it?*

THE MALE ROOM:
Responses from Real Men Who Love Their Wives

What do you love most about your wife's laugh?

CHAD: Her smile and how her eyes light up when she laughs. She puts off a warm aura around her when she laughs, and I like that feeling in the room.

SAM: When I hear or see her laugh, I know she has joy in her heart and she is at peace. Over the last several years, we haven't had a whole lot to laugh about, so to hear her laugh brings a warm feeling over my body.

JACK: That she is happy.

How important is it to you to see your wife happy?

JACK: I rank it right up there with breathing.

CHAD: It is important because it sets the tone in the household. She has the unique ability to handle a situation with one child that requires parental guidance and then turn around to the other children and laugh with them. How can women compartmentalize handling different situations where one instant requires calling a kid out for going down the wrong path and then the next instant requires laughing with your other child?? Men cannot do that (at least I can't). I can't let go of one situation to laugh in another. Must be a gender thing.

SAM: If mama ain't happy, no one is happy!

How often (times a day/week) would you say that you intentionally engage your wife to laugh?

CHAD: I do not think to do this proactively. Makes me feel like a loser now that you mention it. I think this is another item that can get lost in years of marriage. In courtship, we went out of our way to make our future spouse laugh (for attention), now in twenty years of marriage, why do I not put the same amount of effort into it? Doesn't make sense.

JACK: Not enough . . . maybe once a day.

81

SAM: This is an interesting question. I thought I tried to make her laugh in some kind of way every day, but I asked her this question, and she said mostly on the weekends when we are around each other most of the day. I guess that tells me several things right there: I don't spend enough time with her or give her enough attention during the week. I guess I will be adding that to my list of things to do for my wife today.

6

Materialism and the Man

WHEN THE "STUFF WHORES" STEAL YOUR MARRIAGE

Over six hundred underperforming Starbucks closed this year, distressing thousands of ardent users. Apparently, a five-dollar cappuccino brutally bites the budget in this economic climate. Coffee drinkers everywhere are cutting back, resulting in gloomy sales for many of the franchised stores. But even those who are reluctant to pay five dollars or more for coffee are freaking out, begging upper management to discontinue the closings. Why? Because for many Americans, Starbucks represents much more than a coffeehouse—it's home.

Starbucks offers all the tranquility associated with home. At any Starbucks worldwide—whether in Seattle, Paris, or Madrid—folks find a cozy place to sit and read and enjoy a hot, fresh cup of coffee. There's music that carries a "just right" kind of groovy, and the clientele and baristas tend to model exemplary behavior in regard to each other. It's understandable that people everywhere freak when they find their favorite Starbucks closed—they miss the comfort, the closeness, the coffee. You might think it sounds kind of ridiculous if you're not an ardent user, but *The Week* explains the ruckus and the rationale: "Across the nation, desperate customers are petitioning Starbucks management not to shut their favorite 'secular chapel.' It's tempting to mock these disconsolate latte drinkers, but don't. The company's outlets are havens from modern life—quiet, contemplative, and laden with comforting ritual."[1]

"Havens from modern life—quiet, contemplative, and laden with comforting ritual." Sounds to me a lot like home should be. Who could have ever predicted that a coffeehouse would become the iconic symbol of a respite—a haven from modern life?

It's startling but true, and I think there is a reason for it. For many Americans, home has become less of a quiet, contemplative place and more like a pit stop. Whereas Starbucks is the place to meditatively sip your fresh ground extra-foamy, low-fat latte and catch up with a friend, home is the place to hurriedly pour Folgers into a temperature regulated travel mug before you and your family blast into the morning traffic. Whatever happened to home sweet home?

Alexander von Hoffman, a historian and specialist in housing and urban affairs, has a theory. He believes the disappearance of this ideal is a result of a shift for Americans who have moved from seeing home as a refuge and "a sanctuary in troubled times" to viewing home ownership as "an ATM"—mere collateral for more borrowing power.[2] Over the last several decades, homeowners have become quite comfortable with the idea of putting their home on the line to get everything "from new cars to college educations to a home theater."[3] As a matter of fact, they are so comfortable that they overextended themselves and placed their homes in jeopardy. The *New York Times* reports that "Americans owe a staggering $1.1 trillion on home equity loans—and banks are increasingly worried they may not get some of that money back."[4] Not a pretty picture.

It's amazing to think that the American dream of home ownership has become something readily exchanged for a home theater system or a vacation or even a hefty Starbucks habit. We want the stuff so bad that we'll sell our most prized assets to gain them. We're people overwhelmed by the sparkly appeal of the next best thing and the thing we just can't live without— and we're risking our homes just to get it. We're giving away something precious for just more stuff. Like a woman selling her body for a couple of bucks—it's as if we've become "stuff whores." (It sounds harsh, but stay with me and I'll explain.)

The Marital Downside to the Material Upside

You see, not only have we put our homes on the chopping block, but we've unwittingly placed our relationships there too. American marriages bear the brunt of the pain when financial fiascos abound. If it's ever happened to you, I don't have to describe the chaos of being overextended. And I don't have to tell you about the unbearable stress it creates in your marriage relationship. If you and your spouse are anything like me and my husband, then you lash out at each other for poor planning or frivolous spending. And then you spend time imagining that if only you had a more diligent spouse or simply more of the green stuff, things would be much better. It seems clear cut. Obvious.

But according to a recent study, the less obvious issue is the real problem. The real culprit isn't a low-paying job or even those unexpected emergencies. Instead, it's the upsize mentality we bring into our marriage. The author of the study was interviewed by Reuters:

> "For years there has been an emphasis on learning proper saving and budgeting techniques to avoid marital conflict over financial issues," said the author of the study, Jason Carroll, of Brigham Young University in Provo, Utah.
>
> "But our study found that financial problems have as much to do with how we think about money as they do with how we spend money," he added.

After studying 600 married couples who represented a varied ethnic, religious and socio-economic mix, he found about 35 percent reported high levels of materialism and more financial problems than the other couples.

Carroll discovered materialistic spouses put more emphasis on what they have and it took fewer financial problems to cause rifts.

"For a highly materialistic spouse or couple, it takes less financial disturbance to trigger a financial problem. . . . Some would say, 'I'm not living a good life and I don't have a good marriage if we can't afford to go on that vacation or purchase designer decor for our home,' where a less materialistic spouse would not view these limitations as a major issue."

He added that the key to solving financial problems in marriage is to have realistic expectations and to separate needs from wants. By lowering expectations, spouses are less likely to buy unnecessary things and can avoid argument and stress in the marriage. It could also make people more appreciative of what they have.

"We need to rethink the idea that financial problems are always money problems," said Carroll. "We need to start adjusting how much materialistic issues factor into our idea of what makes a good marriage and family life."[5]

I have to tell you, as much as I hate to admit it (because it totally indicts me too), Carroll speaks the truth. Our problem is materialism. We've become a nation of stuff whores and it seems we'll give away almost anything—home, reputation, and yes, even our marriage—to get what we think will make us happy.

It's All Relative

Our problem, in truth, is that we probably don't even understand what materialism looks like. We feel that cutting back from daily Starbucks visits to three times a week is a serious hardship. That paying five bucks for a smoothie at Jamba Juice is a steal of a meal, especially when you can add in a wheatgrass shot for under a buck. (Woohoo, what a bargain.) We think that buying a new sofa on credit without having to start paying for it for twelve months is totally reasonable. And that carrying somewhere in the ballpark of ten thousand dollars on a credit card is "normal." Truth be told, we've had some freewheeling ways for decades.

David Leonhardt, of the *New York Times*, seems to think that the current economic crisis is, well, to put it bluntly, our own fault. "It's your fault. Part of it is, anyway. You, the American consumer, spent too much money. You bought too much house, took on too much debt and generally lived beyond your means. Your free-spending ways helped cause the worst financial crisis since the Great Depression."[6] Thanks for the love there, David. But if that is the case—and we are indeed the generation that has been living this way for decades and the ones who created a national debt that has hit the trillion-dollar mark—we really aren't the ones with the insight to figure our way out of it.

But hopefully there are still some people around who understand what materialism looks like and how to unleash themselves from its deadening stranglehold. Maybe your grandparents or great-grandparents remember when just having a little sugar in their coffee was a serious indulgence. I doubt they would have dreamed of buying food at a restaurant for three times the price that it could easily be made at home. They probably would have scoffed at the idea of buying new furniture when they didn't have money for it, especially when they had perfectly good pieces at home. Because they are the people who not only fought their way through the Great Depression with an unfailing attitude by demonstrating loads of self-control, but they also managed to get through it all with a marriage intact.

As a result of the constant news of our faltering economy, my local paper recently featured three couples, all in their eighties and nineties, who were raised during the Great Depression. Each couple was interviewed about the lessons learned in surviving the most severe depression our country has ever experienced. And all the advice was interesting. But the thing that pinged my conscience the most was the tenderness in the way the photographer captured the couples. They were delightedly hanging on to each other, relishing that they were tucked away at Sun City, a modest retirement community just outside Austin.

When I looked at their pictures, it made me realize that when I near the end of my life, it won't matter how many toys I've collected, how big my house was, or for that matter, even how much of an inheritance I've tucked away for my children and grandchildren. What will matter most is what I did and who I was for the *people* in my life. And mainly, the one person who's supposed to hang out with me forever—my husband.

Raising Your Expectations

So it would seem that the first step toward banishing the stuff whores would be to lower material expectations. In fact, every article I read about capping materialism suggested that very thing. And that will work—if you lower your desire for more stuff. But if I just tell you to stop craving the stuff, that probably won't touch the desire. As a matter of fact, just thinking about not going to Old Navy makes me want to go there and see what's on sale.

No, in this case, perhaps *raising expectations* might be smarter. And I don't mean that you want for more where stuff is concerned. I am thinking that you want for more where your relationship is concerned—raise those expectations. Because if it's true that Americans are more prosperous—and more depressed—than ever, it just stands to reason that maybe we're looking for happiness in all the wrong places.

So what would it look like to raise your expectations in the right direction? To raise marital expectations and lower material expectations?

It starts with getting a marriage mission.

A Mission for Your Marriage

Have you ever stopped to think about why you got married? When I married Will some twenty-four years ago, I wanted love, babies, sex (a tremendous motivation pre-wedding), and to live happily ever after. Will would say his goal was nearly identical—with the exception of the order. And that was good, but honestly, we married for all the wrong reasons. We were hoping to find ultimate fulfillment in each other. To recognize our deepest dreams and desires through each other. And to be elevated to greater fulfillment through each other.

After nearly twenty-five years of marriage, I would say that Will and I have been elevated to greater fulfillment, but not in the ways we originally thought. Instead, we have discovered our marriage mission—and it's all about helping other people.

> Have you stopped to think about why you got married or what you ultimately hope to accomplish in your marriage?[7]
>
> Will Davis Jr.

Now, you might be thinking, oh, of course, you're a ministry couple—that's your job to help other people. But if you think about it from a spiritual standpoint, it's not just our job. It's your job too.

In a nutshell, we're here on planet Earth to fulfill the greatest command: love God and love others. That's our job. And to the extent that we achieve that goal through our marriage, we will find the greatest joy. For Will and me, it truly has nothing to do with "being in ministry." First and foremost, we're full-time Christians—hopefully just like you and your husband. And full-time Christianity equals loving God with all your heart, soul, mind, and strength—and loving others as you love yourself (Mark 12:28–30).

That is what drives me personally, and it's what drives my marriage collectively. While Will and I love each other immensely, we are also out there loving God and others as practically and purposefully as possible. And while doing so, we are fulfilling our mission to love and serve people. And it's in this comprehensive context that we find meaning in our marriage. A meaning that is much bigger than ourselves.

What's Your Marriage Mission?

So maybe you're interested in the proposal of finding your unique mission in marriage. You realize that all the material glitz is getting you in trouble financially. And that the goal of "happiness" or "babies" or even "sex" didn't really end up like you wanted it to. You're thinking that by at least entertaining this idea, you just might end up with a marriage that exceeds your dreams. Well, that's step one—realizing that just maybe there's even more to your marriage than you can see.

> People who give will never be poor.[8]
>
> Anne Frank

But after that, how should you go about defining what your mission looks like? Great question.

First off, the search should be entirely organic. You don't have to suddenly change your personality, sell your house, and drop off the face of the earth. Far from it. It really all starts with what you have in your life right now. Likely, you have several things that could be leveraged for the greater good. You probably have a place you call home, some individual and collective passions as a couple, and hopefully a newfound compulsion to make a difference in others' lives. That's perfect.

I'll give you a few examples of how this has worked in the lives of three very real couples. Take David and Christy May. They've been married fifteen years and have three lovely children. Their two oldest are girls, Madelyn (thirteen) and Courtney (eleven). Both the girls and Christy love riding horses. As a result of David's success in business, they had the opportunity to buy and develop a prime piece of property and open an equestrian center—Lone Star Stables was the result. It's a private barn inside the city limits that houses around twenty horses and trains about forty clients. It's not only a family business replete with the girls scooping out stalls, feeding horses, and doing whatever is needed, but it's also a place where, because of David and Christy's open love of God, people get to hear about Christ in a friendly, relaxing environment. The Mays are also in the early stages of creating a program at the barn to help underprivileged children with autism through equine therapy.

Or another couple, my sister and brother-in-law Linda and Jim Stafford. Their house is perched high above a greenbelt—a lovely, open place to catch a sunset. With almost weekly regularity, Linda and Jim invite people over for a barbeque and sunset watching. It doesn't matter if you're married, single, young, or old—you're invited. Jim fires up the grill for some of the best fajitas in town, and Linda grabs a basketball to start an informal game for those who are up for it. Without fail, people express their unwavering appreciation for Linda and Jim's continual, everyday hospitality.

Or Kevin and Joni Kendrick. They devised a pretty radical, everyday way to live out their marriage mission. After over a decade of marriage with very little desire for children, they saw a story on the news about three siblings who were coming out of foster care and needed a "forever family." Joni and Kevin were so compelled that they decided to adopt them. Now Kevin and Joni wake up and see their marriage mission every morning—in the faces of Kelsey (seventeen), Tyler (fifteen), and Jordan (twelve).

Will and I have a different marriage mission. Ours is more about communication. Aside from founding a church where Will is the senior pastor, we both author books and view publishing (and all that comes with it) as our marriage mission. It includes writing very honestly about our lives and marriage. It includes lots of not-so-glamorous "business" travel away from family when we're promoting the books.

And it also includes an ongoing commitment to granting some grace to whichever of us is in a freakish, frantic writer mode with a deadline.

A marriage mission is about understanding that the union you share is not just about the two of you. Your marriage has a higher calling and a bigger vision—and that can change everything.

About the Joneses: Care, Don't Compare

The idea and implementation of a marriage mission will likely do a few interesting things. First, it will kill the hording, stuff-whore mentality in marriage. Second, it will inspire you to think big and to consider impact. And third, it will also help you see a truth that smacks Will and me in the face daily: people are hurting more than we know.

> How might your marriage be different if you knew that you and your spouse were being used to funnel God's blessings to others? How might your conversations or arguments, spending habits, vacation discussions, and retirement plans change if you both felt compelled to fulfill your marriage's calling?[9]
>
> Will Davis Jr.

I said earlier that Americans are among the richest people in the world—and also experience the highest levels of depression. What's that about? It seems that all the toys don't begin to fuel the spirit. The point here is that excessive materialism is actually an indicator of spiritual hunger. It's a signal that a person feels that they're missing something and they are trying to fill it with the latest, greatest new thing. A hunger-induced sadness.

It's an emptiness that creates a drive for too much retail therapy. When "people devalue themselves and their current possessions, they literally feel worthless. So when given the chance, they're willing to spend foolish amounts of money for new material goods, as a way of enhancing their 'worth.'"[10] If you look at it through a spiritual lens, all the excess materialism and indebtedness simply means that we are around some of the saddest people in the world.

Now that might be a little hard to imagine when you're watching your neighbor cruise happily down the street in his brand-new Beamer, and yet that is just the kind of thing researchers tell us could indicate there is a problem. Those ultra-expensive products are actually a not-so-great way of trying to enhance worth, to relieve emptiness. And this idea that you can drape a new BMW (or whatever) over your life and get some therapy from it is not a new idea; Americans have been perfecting it for decades.

> *Given a choice between taking the day off or keeping a step ahead of the Joneses, it seems outdistancing the neighbors wins every time.*[11]

Instead of trying to keep up with the Joneses (which psychologists tell us is a huge force in materialistic tendencies), why not have some intentional, practical compassion for them instead? Discover your mission and get out there and help some people.

Real Impact

Finally, a successful marriage mission is achieved only through a healthy marriage. For example, it would be pretty insane for Will and me to tour the nation promoting books on marriage if our marriage was a sham. It would be incredibly ridiculous for me to espouse speed sex if I didn't even practice it. Not really the point, you know? It's not that your marriage needs to be *perfect* to successfully have a marriage mission; it's just that it needs to be pointed in the right direction.

Which brings up another point that I'm sure begs for an answer: What if you are married to a man who doesn't grasp or believe the God stuff? What if you are ready to go and impact your world, but your husband, because of where he is spiritually, would smirk and roll his eyes at the thought?

Well then, to be honest, your marriage mission is straightforward. Your marriage mission is to quite literally love that man to God through your example. And I don't mean your example in loving others. That's good and all, but what's really important is that you are an example in how patiently, compassionately, and passionately you *love him*. Simple and incredibly difficult at the same time. Your mission will not be fulfilled through opening a barn, hosting dinner parties, adopting foster teens, or writing books. No, your marriage mission is pure and uncomplicated: love your husband and put him first. You will win him over not by serving everyone else but by serving him.

And that mission, dear friends, is one we should all aspire to.

Uncovering the Truth

- *When thinking of your own marriage, do you see manifestation of some forms of materialism? Who does it impact more (you or your husband), and what do you think is the root cause?*

- *Have you ever considered that excess materialism is actually a reflection of a spiritual hunger? Explain. How about that it's a signal of some soul sadness? Discuss.*

- *How do you think lowering your material expectations could raise the expectations in your marriage?*

- *In developing a marriage mission, it's good to examine what you're already doing as a couple—and how it could be more fully incorporated to include God. What do you and your husband love to do together? How might that be broadened to help other people?*

- *What are three steps you can take to cease keeping up with the Joneses and instead care for the Joneses as a couple?*

THE MALE ROOM:
Responses from Real Men Who Love Their Wives

What do you think are some of the root causes of financial stress in most marriages?

CHAD: Root cause #1—Spending more than we make. I think the biggest root cause of financial stress in marriage (other than I can't win the Pick 6 lottery) is that many families spend more than they make. I think this happens to most people at least once in their life; however, it can be more difficult to fix when you are married. Many times our overspending is tied up in things that cannot be unraveled quickly, such as large mortgages or car payments where it is difficult to sell the item for enough money to pay back the loan or paying for a kid to go to private school (do you really want to take them out midyear?). Root cause #2—Leverage. Borrowing money (you don't have) against credit cards, mortgages, car loans, student loans, home equity loans causes stress. In today's world, it seems we will leverage more via debt before saving more money. Root cause #3—Communication. Many husbands and wives don't want to discuss either how their money is being invested or how it is being spent. The spending discussion (even if you are loaded with money) is rarely a positive conversation, because all of us want to spend money on things that make sense to us as the individual but not to the spouse. For example, does a woman really need a spray-on tan so her legs won't look white when she wears a short skirt? Or do I really need to buy a new golf club to help my less-than-adequate golf game improve? I guess the answer to both is yes.

DAVE: Lack of money. Okay seriously, I think at least part of it is not wanting to appear less than perfect. I am not a good money manager—my wife is a great money manager. I had to get over myself and my own ego to let her do what she is gifted to do.

JOHN: Materialism, being suckers for the pitchman that makes up our economic system, loving the world more than loving the Father, all of which causes couples not to live within their means.

Money issues can cause loads of tension in marriage. What do you and your wife do to keep from letting that kind of stress creep into your marriage?

JOHN: I try to look the other way. *Seriously.*

DAVE: We are very honest about our financial situation with each other. I think there is a huge tendency to try to make things appear better than they are; then when reality strikes it is hard to deal with. When we are out of money, we both know it and revert to tuna fish and are grateful for it. God proved himself to us through a single can of tuna when we were dating, and even now when things get financially tough, we break out the tuna and know he is still with us.

CHAD: Communication. The best thing I have done in our marriage regarding finances is to involve my wife in decisions regarding how we make money. For example, having her involved in decisions regarding which jobs I might consider for my career. Is she interested in me making a lot more money and me being gone from home all the time or making less money and being around the house every evening? Another key area I have her involved in is the discussions on how we invest our money, including retirement. It has taken huge pressure off me to make sure I am making all the right decisions regarding how we invest our money. If things don't work out like we plan, then she was involved in the process. Both of these areas have made our spending discussions much more productive and "friendly." Another, pray. I think this is a great place to insert God into your marriage. Prayer (alone and with your wife) regarding your family's spending, provision, tithing, and investing is a great reminder that God gave you resources to steward and he should be involved with the decisions regarding them.

There are many great books on prayer to help written by a prayer guru named Will Davis Jr.

How is your marriage impacting others in a positive way?

DAVE: We have always felt a calling to befriend those around us and try to serve however the opportunity arises. Sometimes those are couples, sometimes individuals. As we have moved to an "empty-nest" time period, we have felt it important to reach out to families around us and serve as surrogate parents, grandparents, or brothers and sisters. We know what it's like to forge ahead without the aid of family nearby, so we try to make the same situation easier for those around us.

CHAD: We make decisions together on what charities to get involved with and church projects to work on throughout the year. In addition, being aware of the people around you and what is going on in their lives is important. People are hurting more than we could ever know, and asking a few extra questions can uncover lots of opportunities to help someone. The other thing is, we will leverage our relationships and rally other couples around a particular need, such as gathering furniture or clothes for someone whose house has burned down.

JOHN: Numerous invitations to dinner, especially the traditional American Sunday dinner. Sadly, a family tradition that has been lost. We are evangelical in our promotion of this great American/Christian tradition. Like Jesus, we seek to break bread with others, sharing a common meal and conversation.

7

Marriage and Multitasking

DEVELOPING A ONE-TRACK MIND

This information might upset you if you are the type who eats breakfast while steaming the wrinkles out of a shirt, catching the morning news, scanning texts, and asking your husband to take out the trash all at the same time. Apparently, multitasking is making mush of your mind. Scientists have confirmed that the more things you attempt to do at the same time, the less likely you are to do any of them with proficiency. And while there are some things that are effortlessly completed at the same time, like eating and watching television (maybe too easily!), most things in life require more focus, like driving and talking on the cell phone.

Now, maybe you disagree. You feel totally competent driving and talking on the cell phone at the same time and don't think there is much to that at all. But did you know that statistically, if you are doing those two things at the same time, there is an increased chance—by almost 300 percent—of getting in a wreck? That's because driving requires singular focus. And driving is pretty serious business. Though I like to think I can laugh on the phone with my friend Roxann and adequately measure the distance between my car and the one in front of me on the highway during rush hour, I can't. This clearly explains why I almost smashed into someone several nights ago.

> The great irony of multitasking—that its overall goal, getting more done in less time, turns out to be chimerical. In reality, multitasking slows our thinking. It forces us to chop competing tasks into pieces, set them in different piles, then hunt for the pile we're interested in, pick up its pieces, review the rules for putting the pieces back together, and then attempt to do so, often awkwardly.[1]

Don't get me wrong, I'm not advocating that we stop multitasking altogether. But I do think there are just certain things in life that need singular focus—really important things—even more important than operating a car. Like having sex for instance.

Would it startle you to know that 16 percent of people admit to taking a call on their cell phone while having sex?[2] Yes, that's right. Not only are people routinely answering cell phones in crowded planes, dressing rooms, and public restrooms—they're also picking up the phone in bed. Yes, in bed . . . when they're with their special someone *doing that*! Now, not sure about you, but I think that counts for some bizarre form of *mélange à trois*. And you know what? That's just weird. Listen, I don't *want* to talk to anybody about *anything* while they're doing *that*. It's just not that important. And I bet you're probably in hearty agreement with me on that one. But wait, it gets even more peculiar.

Seems it's not just multitasking that's problematic; looks like it's more about the collective obsession we have with techno gadgets in general that's sidetracking relationships. Check this out: 84 percent of those surveyed said they check their BlackBerrys before going to bed and first thing in the morning—and 85 percent wake up and check them in the middle of the night.[3] But there's more: according to a survey of 6,500 professionals, 87 percent said that they routinely take their personal digital assistants into their bedrooms and 35 percent surveyed said they would choose PDAs over their spouses![4] I don't know about you, but I'm wondering what in the Sam Hill is going on out there? That many people would choose a PDA over a spouse?! Just who are they planning on talking to?

The Stressful Sexual Shutdown

We are an electronically inclined nation—and I'm not saying that's necessarily a bad thing. There's certainly nothing wrong with using technology to improve efficiency in our work and home lives. And there's nothing innately wrong with multitasking either. But when technology invades life and multitasking overtakes it, that can create an unhealthy balance—and things can get terribly stressful. So stressful, in fact, that it creates a shutdown.

> A study revealed that eight out of ten adults are so dependent on their cell phones that they can't bear to turn them off during sex.[5]

There aren't many of us who haven't felt the shutdown associated with stress. You get so tired that you're distracted and unmotivated. There's just so much to do and so much to keep organized that you get completely overwhelmed, exhausted by the pace, and end up zoning out on life. The problem with the overwhelm is that, not only is there a shutdown on basic life tasks and emotional well-being, but a new study shows that biologically speaking, women shutdown sexually. Dr. Laura Berman, director of the Berman Center for women's sexual health, says, "When a woman is stressed, the hormonal changes in her body trigger a chemical reaction causing sex hormone–binding globulin to bind with testosterone cells, so they're unavailable for libido and sexual response."[6]

101

To be honest, we probably don't need a study to understand that one. But you might be surprised to discover that for men, it's the opposite. Berman reports that while women go into a "tend and befriend mode when they are under stress" preferring to "nest" rather than have sex, men tend to report a higher sex drive under stress.[7] And that in effect becomes a real problem.

> *Statistics bear out what I'm going to say. What's going on in your sex life is a very good indicator of how the rest of your marriage is going.[8]*
>
> Dr. Kevin Leman

Because the deal is, men typically tend to have a higher sex drive than women anyway, and that further polarizes the differences. While you're stressing about work, the kids, and managing the house, sex is the furthest thing from your mind. But when your husband is stressing, he's feeling more amorous than ever.

Coitus without Interruptus

What you might find hard to believe is that studies show that sex is just the thing you need when you're feeling incredibly stressed. Apparently, psychologists found that when couples engaged in sexual intercourse before a stressful event, they not only lowered blood pressure responses during the event, but those relaxed responses lasted not just for hours afterward but for days.[9] So yes, based on the findings—if you have something really stressful going on—say, oh I don't know, a book deadline is stalking you and you feel like throwing up for fear you won't get it completed—having sex with your husband will not only decrease your stress, but the afterglow will last for days. (Hmm, hold on a sec and I'll be right back. . . .)

Of course, you don't have to trust me and the psychologists—you probably could get your husband to participate in your own little experiment. It's worth a shot, you know.

However, if just having more sex doesn't get you relaxed enough to take it down a notch in your daily life and actually enjoy your husband, I understand. The honest truth is that sometimes I might be willing to give it a shot and try the de-stress sex experiment, but it doesn't touch the angst and anxiety lying deep under the surface. Sometimes (many times) it's far more complex for me. And I know that most of my girlfriends feel the same way.

> There is nothing like uninterrupted cohabitation and grinding responsibility to cast a clear, unforgiving light on the object of desire.[10]
>
> Caitlin Flanagan

I'll *try* to engage my body and my brain. My husband looks cute, smells great, and all that—I'm trying to "be there," but all I can think about is the impending book deadline, the grocery run I should have made yesterday, and fourteen unreturned emails. Argh. The realities of modern life. It's the daily grind for a generation of women just like me who want to have it all—and enjoy every minute of it.

Every Cinderella Needs a Godmother

I think that what we really need most of all is just what Cinderella had—a fairy godmother with the ability to see into the future who can tell us when our carriage will turn into a pumpkin and at what point life will fall to pieces. It would be incredibly helpful to know the precise time on the clock when I will suddenly (metaphorically of course, or uh . . . mostly) transform from being the most beautiful, happy wifey in the world to a sad, stepped-upon, destitute little maid.

It's those magical boundaries I have trouble finding. Between wifing, mothering, home owning, churching, writing, radio hosting, exercising, friending, and basic beautifying—I'm toast. And more days than not, I feel like an overlooked and underappreciated maid—sweatpants, a tired T-shirt, and a dishrag in my hand.

Logically, I know I can't do it all—and yet I still try. And in the trying and all the multitasking—the one person I love the most ends up getting the worst of me. There really is a Cinderella inside me who wants to meet my prince at the ball—who desires the romance, sex, and whatnot—but all too often the magic dissipates before I even know what hit me.

In my hit-and-miss experience, I've found that I must constantly reevaluate my schedule, usually on a weekly basis, so that I can be smart about managing life. Because apart from that, the madness inflicted on my marriage is far too much to take. So just for now, I'm going to impart some of the lessons I've learned. Imagine me as your very own fairy godmother giving you the truth about getting a grip on the stress in your life and your marriage.

Be a Sleeping Beauty

Plain and simple, we need more sleep. Women are notorious for sleepwalking through their days—just packing it all in to please everyone. At some point, you've got to be willing to put down little Billy's preschool project, blow off the dirty laundry, and get in bed at a decent hour. Yes, I know it's hard, but without adequate sleep we can count on lower productivity, lower immunity to illness, and a lower sex drive.

Are you setting yourself up for misery if you don't get your Zs? A new study says that restful sleep makes people happier. On the other hand, poor sleep triples the likelihood of life dissatisfaction.[11]

And on that note, I would add that along with more sleep, we need more rest, which is a very different thing altogether. Rest is what you get when you take a day off to recreate and pull aside from your usual duties. It's about a respite, a Sabbath, a break from the routine. I started designating one day a week for rest over a decade ago, and along with giving me renewed energy during the remainder of the week, it solidified my interest in and attention to my husband and my family. If you are working seven days a week nonstop, then stop. Get off the 24/7 roller coaster and breathe. Your body, mind, and emotions will thank you for it.

Learn to Say No

Whenever I speak to women's groups on the topic of stress and time, I have them say "no" out loud. Amazingly, no matter where I go in the country, the first call for "no" is the feeblest, gentlest little "no" imaginable. I give them fictional situations that are extreme, as in, "Your pastor just called and asked you to head up a volunteer team of five hundred women for a special event the church is hosting in three weeks. It will require a minimum of twenty hours a week—from four in the morning until nine a.m." Then I ask them to give a "no" to the insanity of the request. And routinely what I get is a sea of tiny baby whispers. A minuscule faint "no." After three or four tries, the collective "no" sounds a bit more commanding but not entirely convincing. Women have an issue saying no.

Lack of sleep disrupts every physiologic function in the body. We have nothing in our biology that allows us to adapt to this behavior.[12]

But "no" it must be if you want to have a healthy marriage. Truth be told, most of us have far more opportunities than we could possibly manage. And yet, so few of us plant our feet firmly on the ground and give a strong no to keep our schedule sane.

I love what Stephen Covey has to say about understanding how to make decisions regarding managing a schedule:

> It is not until you have a burning yes inside of you about what is truly important that you can pleasantly, smilingly, cheerfully, say no to all of that which is urgent, but not truly important. Our deepest guilt comes from doing the opposite,

implicitly saying no to the truly important and yes, yes, yes to the urgent that is not important. The more we are free from nonnecessities, the more we are free to do the more meaningful actions of our lives.[13]

Hopefully that freedom from the nonnecessities will equate with meaningful action that communicates our real priority in marriage.

Compensate for Overtime

Another tip that is often overlooked in many busy wives' agenda is making sure that you give overtime to the guy who probably needs it most in your life. If you have an especially crazy week—say the kids had head lice and you're vacuuming the house, washing the clothes at the Laundromat, picking nits out of your kids' heads, and totally grossed out for several weeks on end—be sure to compensate with some downtime with your husband when you get your sanity back. If at all possible, make up for the madness by recouping the losses. Though you can't help what happened or make the nits disappear (dear God, a miracle please), you can push reset on the wifely responsibility as pleasantly as possible when the storm finally passes.

Identify and Manage Your Responsibilities

And finally, realize the importance of your responsibility. It took me a while to get this straight—as simple as it seems. There is only one woman my man is supposed to love body and soul: me. I have to think in terms of identifying what is rightfully expected of me—and what is just an opportunity.

In my marriage, I think it's only fair that Will should expect me to partner with him in raising our kids. That's my responsibility. I think it's fair to be a part of helping overall with the household. That's also my responsibility. And honestly, I think that Will has a right to expect sexual intimacy with me (and vice versa). That, indeed, is my responsibility. So along that line, sex with my husband should not be regarded as an "opportunity" whenever I get around to feeling like it. And though Will is incredibly sensitive about my feelings, I don't want him to think or feel like he has to tiptoe around waiting on my female libido to kick in. And quite frankly, I don't think that I'm a repressed female for expressing it that way.

I have talked with far too many women who think that sex is just something they engage in with their husbands when they have time or aren't stressing about the kids—which is just about never. I remember one cute, stressed-out wife who told me that her husband understood why she had refused him for weeks on end and finished with, "Besides, he can take care of that by himself [indicating masturbation] . . . right?" I was floored.

If the stress—and selfishness—leads us into thinking that a sexless marriage is an option, then we've got a real mess on our hands. Or if we contend that a man who wants to have sex with his wife is a pig, a bigger problem still. The deal is that thinking it's okay/normal for days, weeks, months—even years—to go by without even trying to get it going on is a dangerous, slippery slope for a husband and wife.

Dr. Kevin Leman states it well:

> Marriage revolves around a simple little word called *needs*. As a marriage counselor and psychologist, I'm often asked the secret of a successful marriage. In a world torn apart by divorce, people want to know how to make their marriages work. Well, here's the answer: Become an expert in meeting your spouse's needs. In successful marriages, each partner works to meet the other's needs. Now you should know in advance that you're not going to meet *all* the needs of your mate, no matter what the popular books tell you. You're going to fail at meeting some of those needs. A good spouse doesn't expect the other to bat 1,000. But you need to get the bat off

107

your shoulder, at least. You need to work at meeting a good number of your spouse's needs as best you can.[14]

While I agree that we should meet a man's needs as best we can, I would add that we should also meet their needs *as often as we can.* So whatcha say girls?
Batter up!

Uncovering the Truth

- *Which of the following do you think causes women to feel most overwhelmed and unable to meet a man's needs: working outside the home, the busy schedules of children, or a tight, overpacked family agenda? How might that unintentionally usurp and damage the marriage?*

- *Author Caitlin Flanagan quoted Redbook's online sex therapist, Jane Greer, as saying, "Marriage has changed. In the old days the husband was the bread winner. The wife had the expectation of raising the children and pleasing him. Now they're both working and both taking care of the children, and they're too exhausted and resentful to have sex."[15] Do you agree or disagree? Who is more resentful and why?*

- *Do you think sex is a "wifely duty"? Would it also be a "husbandly duty"? Why is that a paradox?*

- *Where do you think we as women adopt the idea of sex with our husbands as an "opportunity" rather than a "responsibility"?*

THE MALE ROOM:
Responses from Real Men Who Love Their Wives

If your wife says no to your sexual advances, what is the reason most often given?

MICHAEL: That she's too tired.

JACK: It's usually some form of "bad timing."

BEN: Typically, it's just bad timing on my part. She's tired or stressed or just not in the mood.

BARRY: Not feeling well, tired.

What do you think most often stands in the way of sexual intimacy with your wife?

BEN: Quality time. When we're in drive-by mode, it's almost impossible for us to have a meaningful connection on any level, including physical. But when we're able to slow down and really enjoy each other, we're much more likely to connect intimately.

JACK: The kids. They're either in the next room or still awake or breathing or something. . . .

MICHAEL: Busyness.

BARRY: Busyness, too much going on in life, not slowing down enough.

Would you rather your wife meet your sexual needs as best she can or as often as she can? (In other words, quality or quantity where sex is concerned?)

MICHAEL: Yes.

BEN: Is yes an okay answer? Seriously, I love quality sex—the kind of sex where we're both very engaged. I think I'd rather wait for those times when my wife really wants to be sexual than just have her "do me a favor."

109

BARRY: Quality is typically better, but if sex itself has too much time in between times (i.e., weeks) then the quantity becomes an issue.

JACK: Quality . . . I can elaborate here, but you really don't want to hear it.

8

Why Saying Thanks
Is a Big Deal

UNDERAPPRECIATION AND ADULTERY

In his book *The Truth about Cheating: Why Men Stray and What You Can Do to Prevent It*, psychotherapist Gary Newman cites that emotional disconnection is the leading cause of infidelity among men. After surveying married men, he found that over 50 percent reveal that emotional distance from their wives is the very thing that entices them into the arms of another woman.

That surprises me, because I really don't regard men as the type of people who go around focusing on their emotions. It made me wonder if Newman surveyed male poets and songwriters. I just can't imagine my husband leaving for work first thing in the morning, tuning in to a classical station, and driving through traffic untangling his *feelings*. Yes, that might be routine for me, but I am a woman. I consistently replay situations, mull over conversations, and consider how I feel about them. Not so with my guy. Will just isn't the type. And so I felt fairly smug about my husband's immunity to enticement until I read further and found the underlying reason that many men are emotionally disconnected from their wives: they feel underappreciated. And that, my dear friend, scares me.

Now, don't get me wrong. It's not that I don't appreciate my husband—I really do. I think about how glad I am that I married him all the time. About how I appreciate what a fabulous dad he is to the kids. How I am in awe of his spiritual leadership both at home and at church. Nearly every day, I think to myself how lucky I am to be married to this handsome, thoughtful, intelligent, committed, funny guy. It's all up there in my noggin, but for one reason or another I rarely tell him. I keep my little pocketful of gratitude about my marriage to myself.

Now on occasion, I have been known to brag on Will to other people. Like just this morning, to my prayer partner, Jillynn. We have been meeting and praying together for several years, and I am quite sure she knows how grateful I am for Will. I relate stories to her about how Will helps with the kids' after-school practice schedule or comes to my rescue when I need a last-minute grocery run in the middle of preparing dinner. How he drops everything to listen to me verbally diffuse situations when my heart is full and heavy over one thing or another. Of course, the problem is that my knowledge and even Jillynn's awareness of my gratitude is not what Will needs most. He needs to hear from me that he is handsome, funny, and a great dad. And I admit, I just don't tell him enough.

In my very unscientific survey, I have found this to be true in most marriages. My women friends will tell you that they love their husbands and that they express devotion routinely. An "I love you" and a peck on the lips are a part of their everyday existence. But when pressed about actually *verbally appreciating them* with a "You are the best thing that ever happened to me" or a "Have I told you lately how proud I am of you?" a large number admit being ruefully remiss. They just seem to forget to say, "Hey honey, not only do I love you but I appreciate you. Thank you for being such a fabulous provider. Thank you for being so thoughtful and tender toward me. Thank you for helping me with the kids and the dishes and the dogs. You're just the greatest guy in the world. How did I get so lucky to marry a man like you?"

Most wives confess that they simply forget to say what they're thinking, and fail to verbalize their gratitude and miss the chance to build up their man. But by doing so, they unwittingly place their marriage and their man in an unusually precarious place. As a matter of fact, Newman attests that "among all the possible causes of emotional dissatisfaction the most common answer was, 'I felt underappreciated by my wife. She was not sufficiently thoughtful and caring toward me.'"[1] Now, I don't know about you—but that frightens me. Yet startlingly, even knowing that does not always propel me into action.

Like the other day . . .

A Real Mess in the Kitchen

I had just finished researching this whole blasted premise about underappreciation and had contemplated the horror that my husband could possibly feel just like the men Newman researched. The whole concept was floating around in my head as I opened the dishwasher to unload the clean dishes. I was thinking about Will and wondering if he needed encouragement and trying to think up clever ways to deliver—when suddenly, just like magic Will walked into the kitchen. The gentle clinking and clanking of plates and mugs on the granite countertop always brings him instantly into the kitchen. (It's Pavlovian.) I swear to you that this man has completely conditioned himself to drop whatever he is doing the minute he hears me unloading dishes and come help. This was nothing I ever requested but something he does automatically. If Will is home and I am stacking plates, he is there to put them away.

113

So before I could even start thinking about what to thank him for, he was there, as if on cue, providing a reason. And yet something terribly appalling happened. Even though I recognized the thoughtful gesture—and I felt the urgent need to say something—I was silent. In my heart, gratitude surged. I knew I should say, "Will, thank you for always dropping everything when you hear me unloading the dishwasher. It's such a sweet, selfless thing for you to come help me put up the dishes—and especially since I never even ask." But instead I worked silently for several minutes as we moved about the kitchen putting forks and glasses away. And I have to tell you, there was an internal battle going on that I had yet to understand. I was suffering in that silence, wondering what could prevent me from just saying what I was thinking. How could I hold back especially now—knowing that the lack of a "sufficiently thoughtful and caring" attitude could place him in a compromised position? What kind of idiot was I anyway?

Is It Amnesia?

Truth be told, there are days when I feel like I've fallen victim to amnesia. As if I got bopped on the head—just like in a soap opera—completely oblivious to the blessings in my life. Maybe you can relate. Perhaps you have let days or weeks on end go by without ever uttering a word of thanks. It's a fairly common malady—and sometimes it's just about the day-in and day-out wear and tear of life. We get used to all the fine things, like good health and sunshiny days, and we come to expect them as normal. And it's only their absence that makes us realize what we had and what we are missing. It's pretty normal to fall into that mind-set, but it's not particularly healthy. I think that's why God spends so much time in the Bible reminding us to be thankful. I know I need the reminders continually. God instructs us to be thankful—and I have found without gratitude, I am an unhappy negative person.

Not so nice to be around. But the great thing is that forgetting to give thanks where thanks is due doesn't change how God feels about me or determine his course of action regarding me. An imperfect human plus a perfect God is always going to equal grace and mercy and unmerited favor. He is God, after all—never changing, never wavering.

Unfortunately, in a marriage that might not be the case. When you are dealing with two imperfect needy people and one or both are belligerent or oblivious to the other's need for appreciation, ugly things often transpire. That's the frightening part of being in relationships in general. One flawed selfish person, stressed out and working hard, plus another flawed selfish person, stressed out and working hard, sometimes ends up equaling a marriage lacking in mutual appreciation and headed for trouble.

You can imagine how easily it happens. You're busy and he's busy. With a job, three kids, two dogs, and a house to keep up, you're just barely getting by, and it's difficult to take joy in the little stuff. Instead of thanking your husband for helping unload the dishwasher or clean out the garage, you're wondering why in the world he didn't just take care of it himself. I suppose it's because we are situated in a culture full of entitlement, apathy, and general disinterest where encouragement is concerned. Marriage is no exception.

But I have found that even when I'm on my game—spiritual antenna up—I can still neglect to let Will know how much he means to me.

The Sinister Plot: Positioning

You see, what I found in my own life is that so often I really am aware of Will's sacrifice, his selflessness, and his fabulous plate-putter-upper capacity. I think about it every time he walks into the kitchen. So it's not amnesia that keeps me from speaking up and giving Will what he needs. Instead, it's something much more sinister and just as likely to fit into

115

the context of a soap opera. And it's all about positioning, my friend. Mine.

Embarrassingly, I have discovered that I selectively overlook or ignore Will's kindness. When I feel nudged to thank him for helping with the dishes, just as quickly I think to myself, "Well, I *could* thank him, but this really isn't *my job* to put away the dishes—it's *our job*. For heaven's sake, he dirties just as many forks and plates as I do. If I thank him every time he does house chores, then he'll think that he is somehow doing me a favor when in reality, it's his work as much as mine. Everybody needs to pitch in around here anyway." And I remain quiet. Criminally quiet.

I listen to the greedy voices inside my head and end up silent. Then I feel sick and self-satisfied—like I just scarfed down a gallon of Blue Bell ice cream in a dark, walk-in pantry. Guilty as can be, because I am positioning in our relationship with me in mind, not Will. And by that I mean I am thinking about me and how I can further help me. I am pushing my interest to the forefront, making sure that *I am appreciated and helped*.

What I have come to understand is that complimenting and praising someone else is in essence making yourself humble enough to build them up. It's becoming less and less so they can be more and more. It's thinking, "Wow. This person is really something and I am going to promote, extol, and make their deeds known." It's about making something out of what they are doing and who they are—and not so much about what you are doing and who you are. Encouragement is an act of selflessness.

So of course the problem in withholding encouragement when you know that you should dole it out is that you feel small. And that is just how I felt with Will when I refused to verbally appreciate him. Very, very small. That's how I always feel when I know the right thing to do but then I don't do it. When I realize that I should thank Will out loud by pouring praise over the man, but I'm just as dry and contemptuous as ever, I feel minuscule. And as the internal battle rages in my head and I submit to the silence, I spiral downward getting tinier and tinier as I fall.

It's as if somewhere in my head I am erroneously thinking that speaking out will somehow cause Will to fold up and never help with the dishes again. But the truth is, that is severely unlikely. It's actually just the opposite. If I praise him, it will encourage more dish stacking than ever.

Unfortunately, I think I have fallen victim to the lie that by giving something away I might lose a piece of myself. Or maybe it's that I really would like help with the house care and I'm worried that thanking him will create some sense of entitlement on his part. Either that or I wonder if I thank him too much, he'll just want more and more sex. All the reasons are just crazy. They are insanely ridiculous and embarrassing to even speak aloud. But the bottom line is this: it's just rebelliousness. Plain and simple knowing what to do and not doing it.

> Weakness of attitude becomes weakness of character.[2]
>
> Albert Einstein

If you think about it, it doesn't take a rocket scientist to know that if someone does something nice for you, you should thank them, thereby praising their efforts. I do it with abandon where my kids are concerned. With delight for the gal at McDonald's drive-thru when I get my morning coffee. With expressive joy to God when I see his answers to my prayers. But Will . . . not so much. Terrible but true.

So What's a Girl to Do?

Maybe you can relate (or maybe you feel really sorry for my dear husband) and are wondering right along with me what to do about it. Well, I've been thinking long and hard about this and have come to realize what I need to do. I need to stop trying to protect myself, because I am protecting myself at my husband's expense. A problem that is rooted in a colossal misunderstanding—the misunderstanding that marriage should be focused on two people instead of one. Yes, you read that right. Stay with me here, and I'll explain.

If you look at the biblical model of marriage, you will see that God describes the union of two people in marriage as "one flesh." No doubt you've heard it before in a wedding ceremony: "For this reason a man shall leave his father and his mother, and be joined to his wife; and they shall become one flesh." So the dealio here is that, though Will and I are two separate people with separate bodies and distinct personalities, it's our responsibility to understand that our job in our marriage is to prioritize our relationship as "one flesh." Our focus is to be about "we," not "me."

For me, that means I stop thinking so much about myself—and I start thinking about our relationship. It means I come to regard encouraging my husband as a part of building up the "oneness" of the relationship. In a very real sense, I need to understand that when I build him up, I am also building myself up. It's back to that "one flesh" idea. And there's a verse that really nails the specifics: "However, let each man of you [without exception] love his wife as [being in a sense] his very own self; and let the wife see that she respects and reverences her husband [that she notices him, regards him, honors him, prefers him, venerates, and esteems him; and that she defers to him, praises him, and loves and admires him exceedingly]."[3]

In reading this verse, you can see that a man is to love his wife—as his very own self. Then reading further, the text says that a wife should respect and reverence her husband—and implies, as her very own self. It's simply the marriage version of Christ's admonition to love your neighbor as you love yourself.

Break that down into daily life and it looks like this: I notice Will. I regard him. I honor and prefer him. I venerate him. I esteem him. I defer, praise, love, and admire him *exceedingly*. And yes, that means I thank him when he unloads the dishes—*exceedingly*. I get over the rebelliousness of ingratitude. I push aside the internal sinister selfishness. And I speak *out loud* the appreciation.

I just do it.

Practice, Practice, Practice, and Create an Affair of Appreciation

I do want to report that I'm getting much better at this. Just a few days ago, I was writing my hubby an email about Sara's school schedule, and I started it out with a "Hey handsome, just wanted to give you specifics about the schedule and thank you for being so wonderful." I have to tell you that when he came home later that day, he mentioned it. He was kinda surprised by my flirty, affirming salutation, but it certainly made him smile. And it made me smile too—a direct result of the "oneness" thing.

I wish I could give you a pill to swallow or a daily to-do list to build up your husband, but the truth is that you already know exactly how you need to encourage and affirm your husband. If you think about it, you know just the thing to say and do. You're the expert in your marriage and in understanding your man, not me. And it's just a matter of practicing the right thing over and over again until it becomes a habit.

Now at first, you might feel a little freakish about the whole esteem and admire thing. You might be sitting there reading and

> Remember, man does not live on bread alone: sometimes he needs a little buttering up.[4]
>
> John Maxwell

literally racking your brain, trying to figure out exactly how to go about getting to the place where you are an affirming, encouraging wife. No worries, my friend . . . just baby steps.

First, start off with a prayer. Ask God to help you sweeten your marriage with encouragement. Ask him to show you how to affirm your husband. And then start observing what makes your man smile. Not much more difficult than that.

Second, put aside the past. Don't let your past failures (or your husband's) stand in the way of praising him today. I would wager that the majority of praise withheld in marriage is about a reluctance to be encouraging based on whether a wife thinks a husband deserves encouragement. You know what? Determine that you'll be a wife who simply follows God's lead—to love and encourage come what may. Be willing to forget yesterday's irritations and get about the business of living today.

Third, be ready to ban the selfish voices. I promise that you'll hear multiple reasons in your head about why you shouldn't speak up and honor him. Though they might sound incredibly reasonable, I challenge you to think thoroughly about the bottom line. Is excusing yourself from building him up really about him—or you?

And finally, keep in mind that when you encourage and praise your husband, you are building up the oneness of your marriage—and that means that you will ultimately benefit too.

Now, you'll have to excuse me. I need to get busy and have an affair all my own. I think I'll start by telling my handsome husband that he's an exceedingly terrific plate-putter-upper.

Uncovering the Truth

- *Men are often reluctant to admit it, but they need praise. It's a big deal to them. Who do you think is the biggest encourager in your husband's life? Why is it important for you to be the biggest encourager in your husband's life?*

- *As uncomfortable as it is to imagine, author M. Gary Newman contends that underappreciation can lead a man to become entangled in an extramarital affair. With this presumption in mind, how susceptible might your husband be to infidelity on a scale of 1 to 10 (1 being insusceptible and 10 being highly susceptible)?*

- *Why do you think you have trouble encouraging or verbally affirming your husband?*

- *Commit to having an appreciation affair with your husband. Think of five things you could say, write, or nonverbally communicate today to make your husband feel truly appreciated. Write them down and commit to doing at least one a day for the next five days.*

THE MALE ROOM:
Responses from Real Men Who Love Their Wives

How does it make you feel when your wife expresses verbal appreciation for the things you do?

SAM: To me this is the single most powerful thing my wife can do for me. Even more than sex. I know, I can't believe I said that either. To know that she recognizes my efforts and appreciates them gives me strength and confidence. My wife is a very strong woman. For her to verbally appreciate something I have done instead of questioning it or giving advice on how she would have done it (which is very hard for her not to do) would be huge!

JACK: I feel like Mighty Mouse.

CHAD: Good, especially for the things that I do to try and "serve her," such as doing the dishes, folding laundry, vacuuming, making our bed (things I really don't care to do that I don't consider typical "guy" chores).

What is the most uplifting thing your wife could say to you?

CHAD: How much she loves me and that I am the best husband ever, particularly at a time when it would not be expected.

JACK: That I am mighty . . . because I really am sometimes and it's good to hear, especially from your damsel.

SAM: "Make love to me!" And by that I don't mean sex, I mean LOVE! Those four words have so much meaning, so much power! Emotionally as well as physically. Her wanting to get that close and share something that special means that she is proud of me, she approves of me, she believes in me, and she desires me—emotionally and physically. It's an incredible spiritual connection that is so pure, so right.

Ideally, how often would you like your wife to encourage you?

SAM: I honestly believe that if a wife could encourage her husband on a daily basis the world would change! There's so much pressure on a man. God has designed us to be the leaders, and with that comes the pressure. The pressure is either relieved or multiplied by the simple words or actions a wife expresses. They can either be positive or negative, both holding equal amounts of power. Build up or destroy. That is the power a woman has, whether she realizes it or not.

JACK: Every couple of days would be awesome. Especially after a hard day at work or after I "saved the day" by fixing something again.

CHAD: Hmmm . . . I think on a regular basis is good (just not sure if that is daily or more/less often). I think couples who have been married a long time can fall into the trap of pointing out what is wrong rather than what is right because we are moving fast to keep up with kids and schedules (because we are pressed for time we just need something corrected so we can move forward). I would like to see us stop and express true appreciation more, especially when things get hectic.

9

From Roommate to Playmate

DOES YOUR HUSBAND HAVE A GIRLFRIEND?

The moms of Long Island had quite the surprise last year while dropping off their toddlers at a preschool in North Shore. Apparently there was a new Mr. Mom who had created quite the stir. It was none other than the oh-so-yummy Brad Pitt. Yes, that's right. Seems Angelina was shooting a spy thriller in nearby New York City, so Brad had taken over the job of bringing two-year-old Shiloh to school. Now as I'm sure you can easily imagine, it changed things up at the preschool a smidge. No longer were those sleepy-eyed, bed-head moms pulling on any old thing when they dropped off the kids at preschool. No, not at all. A local resident dished all the details: "Brad drives the kids to school, so the moms have started dressing up to drop their kids off. They usually wear sweatpants, but now they're all decked out."[1] Ahem, well, yes.

When I first heard the story, I laughed out loud. I well remember the preschool drop-off days. Rushing around, making lunches, and tying shoelaces for the two-year-old. Getting the dog outside to potty, wiping up spilled apple juice off the floor, and barely having a chance to glance in the mirror. Yes, it was a race against time to get the little ones there on schedule so that you didn't get the scornful but ever-so-gentle nonverbal rebuke from the teacher because you "interrupted the class with tardiness." So to think about these moms being so intentional about getting up early and glamming up because of Brad—well, that's just funny. I mean, first off, Brad has *Angelina*, and second, I'm thinking most of those ladies have a man of their own!

Yes, I could be quite superior in my judgment of them if I hadn't had my own little weirdo wake-up call just a few months ago.

Is That You?

Will and I were headed out to do a book interview for a television show in Canada. We got up at the crack of dawn and headed out to the Austin airport. Now, my wardrobe plan for this plane trip to Canada at 5:00 in the morning was simple: wear comfy, sleepy-type clothes and blow off your hair 'til you get there. You know, relaxed-fit jeans, big roomie shirt, maybe some squishy slip-ons to kick off in the plane, and hair tucked in a big old "chip clip." So that's exactly what I did. My thought was: who in the world am I going to see traveling from Austin to Winnipeg? All I was thinking is, comfort is key.

So we strolled in the airport, checked our bags, whizzed through security (there were like two other people there—that's all), and found the only restaurant that was open that early. After we grabbed some coffee and a couple breakfast tacos, we settled into a comfortable silence as we ate our breakfast.

Just as I looked down, about to take a big old bite of my taco, I heard a faintly familiar voice call my name. And when I glanced up, you could have pushed me over with a feather because standing across the table from us at the Austin airport at five o'clock in the morning was none other than the first guy I ever seriously dated. A guy I considered my first love.

Will recognized him immediately and stood up and shook his hand, greeting him warmly. Then I found my feet and rushed to give him a quick friendly hug. In all, we chatted for about fifteen or twenty minutes. He talked about flying—he's a pilot now. And Will and I talked about our church. And of course, we talked about our families, then caught up on info about his parents and mine. It was really good to see him. Truly. But I have to tell you, all I kept thinking about the entire time he stood talking was, *Note to self: Never wear comfy clothes to the airport! It might be the one time you see your old boyfriend for the first time in years! Wake up, Susie!! Wear cute, sexy jeans. Cute, sexy shoes. And by all means, don't wear bloaty, formless T-shirts! Hello!!!!*

Now all that internal panic might sound funny to you, but it seemed entirely reasonable to me. I mean, here I am at the airport at an entirely unreasonable hour, and I just happen to see my old boyfriend for the first time in years, and I look like someone who needs to be on *What Not to Wear*. Gracious, Susie, really?!?

When the conversation ended and he strolled off to do his piloting, the internal dialogue ceased. And just as it did, I looked up at my husband of twenty-four years and thought, *Ahhh. I love that man—thank goodness he doesn't care what I look like.* And just as I did, I realized the irony of what had taken place. Here I was frumping in the airport with the man I love, the man I chose to spend my whole life with, as if he didn't matter near as much as a brief sighting from an old boyfriend. It was time to wake up!

Being Too Comfy with the Closeness

I'm not quite sure when we get *so* close that we get *too* comfy, but it does happen in most every marriage. (It obviously had in mine.) At some point, whether a couple has been together

127

a year or ten years, it seems there is a collapse of care that creeps in. The once cute newlywed, instead of caring how she looks, gets a little too comfy with the closeness and blows off her appearance. The process is usually very gradual, without fanfare, and goes unmentioned. It seems to happen slowly at first, but then suddenly you're just not who you thought you were. Or probably even who your husband remembers.

I mean, think about it. When dating, you wouldn't have dreamed of coming to the door to greet your boyfriend in what is now standard wifey wear. But with the kids, a job, and a house to keep up with, it's just overwhelming. And there's no reason to dress to impress. After all, you snagged your man years ago—what does he expect? The little woman greeting him at the door in a dress, heels, and bright red lipstick? Give me a break.

And yet I fear that when the closeness creates an absence of care in the course of marriage, it's not just our husbands who lose out, we wives also lose something that matters in the long run. That just maybe, if I'm more concerned with how I look when I happen to see an old boyfriend at the airport than about pleasing the man I'm married to, I've lost an important part of who I am.

Being a Good Girlfriend

Think back with me if you will to the time when you were dating around, on the lookout for Mr. Right. Come on . . . think back, think back. Yes, that's it. Now remember what it felt like to get the call from *the guy*. You know, the guy you were just *dying* to date. He calls, you flirt on the phone a bit, and then he garners the nerve and asks you out. You willingly accept, and then after you hang up, you commence gathering ideas on what to wear. You go to the closet, rummage through your best jeans, eye a pair of strappy sandals, and then start the search for the perfect shirt and accessories. Yes, that's the one—whew, you found it.

Of course, between the phone call and the day of, you switch your outfit around endlessly. And even when you finally decide, completely certain of the pick, you wonder if you should have gone out and charged up a storm to get something completely new. But suddenly, the day has arrived. The doorbell is ringing, and you're ready to meet your dream date at the door.

You answer the door, he steps in and hugs you hello. From just the brief hug, you notice he smells *really great*. A bit off guard, you laugh and pull away to coyly grab your sleek little purse on the entry table. When you walk outside and turn to lock the door, you feel his glance on your back—and you turn around to give him a quick, smart smile. As he walks you to his car and opens the door, you wish for a touch more lip gloss but don't want to seem like you're trying too hard, so you sit still, though slightly uneasy. He finally gets in the car and starts the engine, and you're off for three hours of anxiously trying to read and impress Mr. Right. See, the thing is, you really like him, so you just want to be the *perfect girlfriend* prototype. Friendly and flirty, but not too clingy. Funny and fresh, though not obnoxious. But most of all, you want to figure out what it takes to make the two of you a perfect match.

If you were even barely able to remember those kinds of feelings, then you remember what it's like to try and be the kind of girl a guy could enjoy being with. And if you recall with any clarity the early years of dating your husband, you likely remember what it took to make a good match with him. I know I do—and frankly, she's a long way away from that girl he escorted to the airport that morning. A long way.

He Doesn't Need a Roommate

Being a good girlfriend to your husband isn't rocket science. Yet somewhere in the dreariness of day-in and day-out living, we lose the sizzly edge in our marriages. What with bills to pay, children to raise, and in-laws to entertain, we forget the fun of being married to the man of our dreams. And suddenly we slip from being somewhat of an ideal kind of marital playmate (and I do mean in both senses of the word) into a bedhead kind of roommate.

The marriage shuffles along with the both of you managing kids and a house and a life but missing a mojo component. As a matter of fact, the marriage feels more like a business arrangement—a flurry of who picks up which kids when and a chore list on the refrigerator door. On any given day, you could find the kids tucked in bed and you in your favorite ratty pajamas next to your husband in bed, where he sits reading some big fat something from work. In a matter of minutes, you both drift off to sleep to catch z's—to do it all over again in the morning. And although there is some kind of familial coziness to that—you gotta admit, it sounds more like roommates.

For many couples child rearing has become not merely one aspect of marriage, but its entire purpose and function. Spouses regard each other principally not as lovers and companions, but as sharers of the great, unending burden of taking care of children.[2]

Caitlin Flanagan

But that need not be so. Turning your marriage around in this area is within reach. It's really just about understanding and valuing what might be important for your husband where your relationship is concerned. If he's an average guy, he probably still enjoys appraising your body. He probably still appreciates when you dress up for him. I'm sure he'd love for you to notice him when he comes in the door at the end of the day. And no doubt, a little flirting would be great.

If you want to change from roommate material to playmate material, it's just not that hard to do. And it's never too late to learn. As a matter of fact, you more than anyone else hold the keys to unlocking the magic with the man you married.

It's really just a matter of restarting some of the behaviors that got you two together in the first place.

Step One: Dress the Part

Now honestly, I really have to work on dressing the part of the cute girlfriend for my husband. It's not that I don't care what I look like—because I can actually be quite vain. For example, I won't leave the house without makeup on and I rarely trip around town in a baseball cap (though they can be absolutely adorable). But somewhere down deep inside, I have developed a little Austin-style hippie blood in my veins. It's not actually a bad thing. I do, however, need to distinguish that there's hippie chic—really cute— and there's hippie casual—which only looks cute if you're a university student. And I must admit that I have been known on more than one occasion to be hanging out in hippie casual. For me that means riding at the barn and then running around town in super-grubby jeans, a "Life is good" T-shirt, black Old Navy flip-flops, and not-so-great helmet hair. Kinda bleak—especially at forty-five.

Though I'm grateful to live in Austin, where things are relaxed and casual, I realize that I need to put a little more effort into cute-ing up for my husband. As a matter of fact, seven out of ten men surveyed said they were emotionally bothered when the woman in their lives let herself go and didn't seem to care about making an effort to do something about it.[4]

> Call me naïve, but I just didn't realize that the issue of appearance was such a big deal—such an imperative deal—for a guy. Important, yes. Imperative, no. Of course, having learned just how visual men are, I should have gotten a clue. But somehow I assumed that if I was out of shape, I was the only person who was negatively affected.[3]
>
> Shaunti Feldman

131

My Will? Well, he's never complained. He's actually the greatest ever, because he has *never* complained about my barn attire. Not once. Maybe the same way that your husband has never given you grief about your excessive sports bra addiction. Or your Winnie the Pooh pajamas. Or your "the baby barfed on my shirt this morning and I never had a chance to change" T-shirt. I know, I know—our husbands are the greatest.

> *The steady dripping of rain and the nagging of a wife are one and the same.*
>
> Proverbs 27:15 CEV

And because of that, I say that we should be the greatest right back at them with a little more mindfulness about dressing the part of the knockout girlfriend. That might mean doing some shopping for new jeans and shapely shirts. Or perhaps it might mean making that appointment to get your hair trimmed or your nails done. I don't know, it might even mean getting a little more serious about taking care of the bod by working out and eating right. It all matters when you begin to care what you wear.

Step Two: Overlook the Fine Print

While step one is primarily about how we look, step two hits squarely in the "what we say" category. So just to illustrate, let me ask you a question: Did you ever hear about the artist who designed a Christmas ornament for the White House tree while Bush was in office? Apparently, her abhorrence of the president was so great that she painted minute verbiage on the ornament, demanding his impeachment. The words were completely disguised in an inventive pattern. The artist had hoped that no one would notice, in an attempt to "get one by" the administration. But I love what Laura Bush decided to do about that angry ornament—she left it hanging on the White House Christmas tree and decided to simply "ignore the fine print."

Now that's an ingenious idea. And one that would be well utilized when the man in your life is driving you crazy. Because at one time or another, being a good girlfriend to your husband will mean that you have to ignore the fine print and keep your mouth shut. Maybe he forgot to take out the trash. Or perhaps he left his dirty socks sitting on the couch after watching several hours of ESPN. The fine print erupts in all our marriages at one time or another and it's tempting to scream. But . . .

If you're busy being the good girlfriend, you'll overlook the fine print and keep it quiet. (Was there fine print back when you dated? I imagine yes, but it probably didn't get under your skin.) You'll let the irritations slide without a lecture. And you'll remember that we've all got some irritating habits that annoy the ones we love the most. But what we never want to do is let the irritations rule or set a negative tone in the relationship.

Because you see, I fear if we don't ignore the fine print, then that could lead us to those weird psycho girlfriend tendencies. You know the psycho girlfriend—a compulsive, controller nag who hounds her poor husband to death? The gal whose every breath spews a complaint. No affirmation. No admiration. Just excessive projectile-type correction. Not a good girlfriend at all.

When the daily irritations impact the relationship and we zealously hone in on the irritating fine print, we inadvertently start exercising the exact opposite of what we most want to be. We act worst with the ones we love the most.

Be the ultimate first lady—and determine to ignore the fine print.

> *For my own amusement, I took to counting the seconds between arriving home from work every day and the first negative comment. It was generally significantly less than a minute.*[5]
>
> Anonymous male
> in his fifties

Step Three: Date Your Mate

Finally, step three: girlfriends should expect a date now and then. Now, it's likely you've heard all the warnings about the need to set aside a weekly date night. And if you indeed are that couple who makes it happen week in and week out—congratulations! That's amazing! Permission granted to skip down to the bottom of the chapter and check out what The Male Room has to say. But . . . if you're like me and you've struggled to manage a date night with your husband, then read on.

The importance of investing in your marriage cannot be overstated. At the end of the day, there is nothing more important than you and your husband as a couple—without the kids. Your marriage relationship is the bedrock of your family. Without "couple" stability, a family is in danger of not only stagnating but breaking.

While it's easy to believe that it's just too stressful to be away from the little ones or find a way to pay a babysitter, it's way more stressful drifting apart for lack of connection. I like what Gary S. Shunk, a Chicago therapist, says about the importance of a date night in marriage. He advises couples to go on dates, to spend time and money together. He says, "What it does is enliven the marital foundation. It's a kind of investment into the heart and soul of the relationship."[6]

If you think of dating as an investment in marriage long term, then it stands to reason that you can't wait several years (or more) to add to the account. If you want to make it to retirement, you've got to put something in now to have something worthwhile much later. And listen, even if you can invest only tiny pieces of time alone together—like maybe sneaking off to a coffee shop for thirty minutes or so—go for it. That's certainly better than nothing at all.

It's not too late. Take the time to work on your relationship. Jump in and start to enjoy the things you used to do together. And if you happen to have a reluctant Romeo, then all the more reason to be a good girlfriend and do something you just know he would enjoy—like maybe attend a college basketball game. Or maybe entice him to catch an action flick at the theater (there's always the popcorn, or if you're really tempted you could try making out—I bet that would please and surprise him). It's not too late to sit in a deer blind. Or scoot the kids to your sister's for the night. Not too late to make dinner reservations at your favorite restaurant. Never too late to go on a business trip with him (you lounge around, just waiting for his return to the hotel room). Or if you're the type who likes camping, well then, it's the perfect time to pack up the camper with a new negligee and some hot dogs and beans.

It's just never too late to be a good girlfriend to your husband. Move from roommate to playmate. All it takes is a little ingenuity and a lot of love.

You go, girlfriend!

Ask yourself: what did we used to have fun doing together? Whether it's listening to live blues or playing putt-putt golf, try it again. A lot of times those activities have leftover magic in them. They serve as poignant reminders that yes, before you were scraping teething biscuits off your sweater and organizing his sock drawer, you were one half of a romantic, swooning twosome who could hardly keep their hands off each other.[7]

Lorilee Craker

Uncovering the Truth

- *Have you ever found yourself more concerned about how people other than your husband felt about how you dressed? What does this stem from?*

- *Think back to when you were not married and dating. What were some of the things that made the good girlfriend list? What about the bad girlfriend list?*

135

- *Why do you think we stop thinking of ourselves as girlfriends when we start thinking of ourselves as wives? Should some qualities cross over? Which ones?*
- *Plan out four date nights for the next four weeks. Try to be as diverse as possible. Be sure to note which dates were most successful and why. Repeat.*

THE MALE ROOM:
Responses from Real Men Who Love Their Wives

What is your wife wearing when she looks most attractive to you?

BEN: Typically, a smile. It doesn't matter how she is dressed. If she is happy and joyful, then she is absolutely beautiful. But if she's griping or prickly, then it can quickly kill any potential romantic spark.

JOSH: Party clothes: blouse, pants, and fun jewelry, comfortable shoes. Hair not too fancy.

SAM: Honestly, it's absolutely nothing. I am so attracted to my wife when she is totally naked. Her body is getting better every day! She's like a very fine bottle of wine. She takes great care of herself, and that is incredibly attractive. A very close second would be her workout clothes, hair in a ponytail looking all athletic!

If/when your wife corrects you, how does that make you feel?

JOSH: If my error is relevant to others understanding the conversation, then I'm happy for it, but if it is nitpicky, mean-spirited, or a one-upsmanship, then it makes me mad and embarrassed.

BEN: It all depends on how and when she offers the correction. If she gets "permission" first—if she tries to understand where I am and how prepared I am to hear her correction, then I'll receive it and grow from it. But if she just dumps it on me—more in an effort to get something off her chest than to help me—then it can be really hurtful.

SAM: Inadequate, stupid, insecure. I married a very strong woman. I don't think she realizes it, but the way she corrects me is very humiliating and deflating. She always has a better way to do it. Don't get me wrong, I need correcting sometimes, but there is a way to correct your spouse without creating tension and animosity.

137

Describe one of the best dates you and your wife ever went on.

SAM: Wow, we've had a bunch of great dates, most of them just sitting in a restaurant talking for hours on end. But a very special one that comes to mind is when we were in Hawaii, we enjoyed a day on the beach, and that night we had dinner reservations at a nice seafood restaurant. We had a great candlelight dinner and sat and talked for several hours. After dinner we were heading back to our room and there was a guy playing the piano and singing, we stopped and sat down and just listened to him. The ocean was in the background, the sun had set, and it was incredibly romantic—it was like he was singing to both of us. Didn't have to say anything, we just sat there with her in my arms and our feet up, so relaxed, so peaceful. A moment filled with peace and joy with the one you love.

BEN: We spent two days staying in a hotel about fifteen minutes from our house one anniversary. We saw two or three movies, enjoyed long dinners, went for walks, ate ice cream, and had a great time. We both hated to see it end.

JOSH: We dressed up for a dinner with some friends that turned into a pub crawl and then into dancing at a disco until four in the morning followed by breakfast at Magnolia Café—an all-night diner. The night wasn't too expensive, she didn't complain about my dancing, and we laughed until we were hoarse. We still made it to church the next day!

10

The Difference between Cats and Dogs

AND OTHER MARITAL MYSTERIES

Read this: Women are hard to read. Seems everyone agrees that women are a tad difficult to figure out. In a recent study, researchers at Indiana University showed video clips from twenty-four different speed dates and had participants answer two simple questions: "Do you think the man was interested in this woman?" and "Do you think the woman was interested in this man?"[1] Then they compared the responses with the speed daters to see if the participants were able to accurately assess interest. On the whole, the participants gauged the man's interest with precision while they were completely mystified trying to gauge a woman's interest. So everyone agreed: women are hard to read.

It's funny that they needed a study to verify the obvious. That it took a team of researchers analyzing video footage to understand what really seems plain as day. And yet, I can appreciate their enthusiasm in further unraveling the mysteries between men and women. Because even after twenty-five years of marriage, I still seem to get a revelation every now and then about the chasm that separates women and men.

As a matter of fact, I often think that writing these marriage books is some kind of grand plan from God for me alone—so that I will be better able to understand and love my husband. Because truly, this manuscript is a lot like a dissertation fraught with evidence gleaned from perusing hundreds of articles and from a little personal research too. My lab results are not nearly as clinical as what you might find at Indiana University, but I actually think they are quite viable. Much of my experimentation is done right here in my own home (bless Will's heart—he's my guinea pig), but some of it is accomplished just by observing and talking with the men in my world.

Studio Study

So far this year, the biggest eureka moment outside my home laboratory came when I started a new job as a DJ about nine months ago at a radio station here in town. For the first time in my life, I was tossed into really tight working quarters with a man. And though I've had male co-workers in the past, it was always in a situation that allowed for more breathing room. Literally. Not so with the radio gig. Every weekday morning it's me and Roxanne and Gary working in a studio about the size of a large walk-in closet. We are metaphorically trapped in there by the microphones and other equipment, sitting and talking it out, only inches apart till the show is done some three to four hours later. And it is in that studio that I have observed some of the most helpful and recent pieces of man data to date.

The fact that I am sitting across from a real man's man all morning coupled with the fact that he literally could be my husband's twin (per his manliness quotient) is a boon for me. The reality hit me square in the face just a couple months after I started. I had my face buried in my laptop, completely engrossed in scanning the news when I heard something awfully familiar. It's a noise that is quite difficult to describe but sounds a little like what I imagine is the squawking of an adolescent eagle.

I heard the noise and glanced up, amazed to see Gary yawning, stretching his arms out as far as he could making this eerie eagle sound. Dumbfounded, I uttered a "Wow." He glanced over at me without the slightest self-consciousness and said something like, "You gotta really stretch with those good yawns." And then he went back to work. I stared at him for a moment, mentally integrating this new information with an older "Will" file I had stored in my brain.

What I found is this: Gary and Will yawn identically. They stretch with wild abandon no matter who's around, arms at full span. They release a loud, guttural eagle cry midstretch. And when they're done, they act as if nothing happened. It's a man yawn.

Now, two things came out of this studio study for me. First, I realized that this yawn of Will's (that had always been a real irritation to me) was actually quite normal for a man holding Will's and Gary's size manliness quotient. Second, I realized that while I would never criticize, scold, or correct Gary for his yawning style, I had routinely criticized, scolded, and corrected Will for his demonstrative ways. In that moment I realized that, though inadvertently, I was indeed trying to meld Will into something he's not and something I'd never want him to be—and that is, a lot more like me.

It's when I forget to recognize those obvious male-female differences and celebrate them that I try unconsciously to turn my husband into something more like a girl than a guy. When I censor his loud yawning or cap his heavy stomping around the kitchen first thing in the morning, I'm actually indicating that it'd be better if he were just a little less masculine. More quiet, more discreet—and well, more female. (Do you know any women who screech like eagles when they yawn?)

141

But that whole premise is way off the mark. We are created differently on purpose, and that purpose actually enhances our marriage. Men need to act like men and women need to act like women—that's good for men and women (wives included). And though integrating those differences can be difficult at times, it's the resulting combination that makes the marriage what it's meant to be. It's exactly what God had in mind from the very beginning.

I love how psychologist Kevin Leman puts it:

> We have a Creator who knew how to put the earth in outer space on exactly the right axis. One degree this way and we fry. One degree that way and we freeze. So don't you think he knew what he was doing when he made men and women? You should be thanking God that your spouse is different from you. Your mission for your entire marriage—not just during dating or in those euphoric first couple years—is to get behind your spouse's eyes and see how he or she looks at life. It's not the lighting of the unity candle that magically makes you become one. Becoming one is a daily working out of your relationship.[2]

So how do you "get behind your spouse's eyes"?

Say What You Need to Say

One of the most important places to "see" what your guy sees is in the area of communication. That's where the thrust of the differences begins. Not only do we use way more words than men to express ourselves, we women are physiologically more adept at communication. Dr. Leman adds a great word picture to his explanation:

> Did you know that scientific studies prove why a woman tends to be more "relational" than her male counterpart? A woman actually has more connecting fibers than a man does between the verbal and the emotional side of her brain. That means a

woman's feelings and thoughts rip along quickly, like they're on an expressway; but a man's tend to poke slowly, as if he's walking and dragging his feet on a dirt road. Eventually his thoughts will catch up with the woman's, but it may be miles down the road.[3]

It's not that men are inferior where communication is concerned, any more than a woman is inferior where physical strength is concerned. But the truth is that the physiological makeup of men and women requires that we handle certain tasks differently because of our inborn distinctions. And while it's easy to *see* the obvious physical muscular structure of men versus women, it's not as easy to see those emotional communication structures. But it's something that a thoughtful wife needs to keep in mind all the time.

Women usually have it a little easier where emotive communication is concerned; therefore, we need to think about how to effectively communicate so men can hear. Rick Johnson wrote an entire book, *The Man Whisperer*, on learning to speak a man's language. He suggests that there are ten keys to successful communicating with a man. I'll list them here:

Give him space—prep him ahead of time and give him a day to think things over.

Simplify—get to the point in thirty seconds or so.

One topic at a time, please—stick to one topic at a time and let him know when you're changing topics.

Be consistent—keep your communication behavior the same.

Say what you really mean—men think literally, so speak literally.

Give him a problem to solve—if you want cooperation, ask him to solve something instead of just talking about it.

143

Get physical—allow for talk while he's puttering or working with his hands. The conversation will be much more productive.

Timing is everything—find a time to talk when he's not exhausted—as in not when he walks in the door at the end of the day.

Fight fair—don't take to heart what a man verbalizes when he's upset because in many cases, he simply doesn't think ahead about what comes out of his mouth.

Speak plainly—men aren't mind readers, so tell him up front what the conversation goal is and help him achieve it.[4]

If that list seems too long to remember, too hard to compile, do this: Practice what I've had to learn to do on the radio in those teeny tiny spots between a song and an ad. Avoid excessive storytelling and rabbit chasing—pretend you have only three minutes of your husband's attention (because in actuality, you just might), and communicate as if he can't even see you. Just trim it down, get to the point, and say what needs to be said. Works like a charm.

Consider His Intent

At times it might be hard to believe, but your husband is not intentionally trying to drive you crazy. I remember a time when Will was just taking me to my wits' end, and in desperation, I picked up a book by a psychologist that seemed to be on his game. He said that if you'll only politely remind your partner of things that bother you (he actually suggested each spouse make a list!), then they'll adjust the behavior and discontinue. I thought to myself, *Gosh . . . that's so rational. I'll try it.*

So the next time Will left his jeans lying by the bed in front of the closet, I reminded him, "Will, would you mind hanging up your jeans instead of leaving them lying here next to the closet? It bothers me and I just wanted to remind you that it's annoying to me." Now, the great thing is that he responded enthusiastically, "Oops. Sure. I'll hang them up. Sorry about that." And with that, I thought the problem was all but eliminated. What was I thinking? I should have known better.

Within days, once again . . . jeans lying on the floor next to the closet door. So again, I tried the psychologist's trick. And again, a sincere apology with a promise to make things better.

Well, I don't have to tell you that it was only a matter of days before it was round three—the same thing. It was so completely irritating to me in a new and different way because I had *asked Will so nicely* to please stop annoying me with this random little habit. I had followed the doctor's orders, for heaven's sake. And

When I say things, I mean them. I like to say what needs to be said plainly. But when I'm quiet, I'm hoping you get the drift that I'm not crazy about what you're saying, but I don't want to hurt your feelings. I'm a tough guy . . . but I'm tender underneath, especially where my family is concerned. Truth is, I'm no big puzzle. And neither is any man. We men and Simple Simon have a lot in common. The path to our heart is well marked, but it's also narrow, for there are few that we trust with it. Because for a guy, sharing your heart can be awfully risky.[5]

Dr. Kevin Leman

just as I was good and ready to really make a case out of the situation, I had a twinge of truth pierce my conscience. I realized what I already knew: Will wasn't *trying* to drive me crazy. He really wasn't.

And in much the same way, I am not trying to annoy Will when I point out available parking spaces when he is driving. I am not trying to push him over the edge when I forget to replace the toilet paper. And I certainly am not trying to drive him insane when I talk to him endlessly in bed before sex.

The plain and simple fact is that as much as we love each other, we routinely drive each other bonkers. And that fact makes it necessary for me to exercise an overriding principle so that I don't let the little things, like jeans lying on the floor, pull us apart. The principle: it's quite difficult to pick the splinter out of Will's eye when I have a two-by-four in my own. Or put another way, instead of making a fuss about all the little things that Will does that make me less than happy, I need to concentrate on those things that I do that create unnecessary friction in our marriage. I must extend grace to my husband—the same kind of grace that God has so willingly extended to me. Because when I manage to extend grace to Will over whatever habit might be grinding on my nerves, I make God quite happy.

As with physical allergens, the first exposure produces a small negative reaction, but each subsequent contact increases sensitivity. That is why those in long-standing relationships can explode over what seem like tiny infractions. The first wet towel on the bathroom floor is mildly irritating; the hundredth can unleash a hypersensitive reaction. Then there are the behaviors you've talked about ad nauseam but persist. If it seems like your partner just can't change this aspect of himself, it's time to take stock. Try reminding yourself what you have—and what you stand to lose.[6]

Jay Dixit

Embrace His Simplicity

And finally, my grand observation regarding men and women and sex and marriage? Here it is: men are like dogs and women are like cats. And the two are completely different!

Until recently, I never really appreciated the stark difference between cats and dogs. I grew up in a family that had only dogs. As a matter of fact, we were such dog people that I was somewhat of a cat hater. That is until Madeleine came along. About two years ago, a little black and white tuxedo kitten wandered into our garage. The minute I saw her, I explicitly instructed my youngest, Sara, to shoo her back out to the streets where she would find her way home. Long story short, not only did that kitten refuse to leave our property (apparently this is how cats work—*they choose you*), but we managed to take her pitiful little self in under the precept that we would

> Honor God by accepting each other, as Christ has accepted you.
>
> Romans 15:7 CEV

find a good home for her. Within just a couple of days, she had weaseled her way into our hearts. Madeleine has become my most favorite pet ever. I love her more than any dog I ever owned.

Madeleine, however, is a real priss butt. She is selective in her desire to see me, will not come when called, and will allow petting only when she feels like it—thank you very much. Though she is soft and silky and completely enticing, she is aloof and moody and what some might call tricky. She might seem to be coming toward me for affection, but that desire can be easily undermined with the flip of a switch or a passing fly or any other thing that comes to mind. I have stopped trying to count on her. She is completely unpredictable. It all just depends.

Our black lab, Mike, on the other hand, is the most fabulously uncomplicated animal I've ever known. Though now aged and arthritic, he will rise to greet me while wagging his tail no matter what time of the day or night. He is faithful and loyal and always on call. There is never a time when I am uncertain how he feels about seeing me.

In my opinion, these two examples are completely applicable to unraveling one of the most challenging differences men and women face: our approach to sex. In general, men are faithful, loyal, and always "on" when it comes to sex. As a matter of fact, I am betting there is never a time a man is uncertain about how he feels about having sex. Conversely, women are

147

> *Men have a lot in common with cocker spaniels and golden retrievers. They all need to be stroked. And if you stroke them, they will reward you with loyalty for a lifetime. Their eyes will not wander to anyone else. They will come trotting happily to your side as soon as you call.[7]*
>
> Dr. Kevin Leman

usually soft, silky, and completely enticing but aloof, moody, and what some might call tricky in regard to sex. They might desire it but can be easily undermined with the flip of a switch or a word carelessly spoken. It's all a little unpredictable and . . . it all just depends. Yes?

I don't mean this in a demeaning fashion at all, but think about it—men are pretty simple. When Will flirts with me, nine times out of ten he's thinking about sex. On the other hand if I flirt with Will, things just might be a tad more complicated. I might be interested in a quick tryst, but it's just as likely that I am only trying to be cute and the thought of sex hasn't even crossed my mind. If I appear amorous though, he'd better jump at the chance, but if he comes on like gangbusters, my response might not be so eager. Because you never really know with cats.

So I suggest you look at your sex life through puppy dog eyes. As a simple gesture of love and affection. There's never a time when my dog Mike gets up to see me when I won't give him a pat and love on him. So if I am willing to do that for my black lab, Mike . . . well, I certainly should be willing to do the same for my man.

Marital mysteries will always abound. But in this case, I think if you can't teach an old dog new tricks, then the responsibility rests squarely on the kitty cat.

Uncovering the Truth

- *Is there a chance that, even after years or decades of marriage, your husband would say you are hard to read? What about the reverse?*

- *What would you say makes seeing life like your husband sees it difficult?*

- *How has observing other men helped you understand your husband better?*

- *What is the thing your husband routinely does that drives you crazy? Do you truly think that he does it intentionally? What is your best reaction to this?*

- *Think of a pet you love or loved immensely. Would you say that your husband receives the tender care that you give to that pet? What about the affection?*

THE MALE ROOM:
Responses from Real Men Who Love Their Wives

Please list what you think are the three biggest differences between men and women.

BEN: 1. Emotional abilities. Men tend to be stuck in an emotional rut. 2. Word count. Need I say more? 3. Sexual wiring—women need a reason; men just need a place.

JOHN: 1. Physical strength. (This has real implications in the relationship between men and women historically and even today.) 2. Emotional makeup. 3. Child care.

CHAD: 1. Problem solving—women will tend to discuss a problem and how to solve it with others, taking into consideration those affected by the solution. Men are not necessarily focused on how the problem is solved (regardless of who is affected) but how effective the resolution is and how quickly it can be solved. 2. Thinking—I think women tend to think about a number of problems at one time while men tend to focus on one or a few problem(s) at a time. 3. Men forget everything, women remember everything. 4. Women are emotional and men are physical.

JACK: Estrogen . . . testosterone. Women "feel" it, men "see" it. Women are pretty, men are ugly.

What is the one thing your wife routinely says or does that makes you crazy, and why?

JOHN: My wife used to be careless with money. I was working my butt off for the family, earning money through self-denial, stress, labor, and she spent it carelessly (this could even be not comparative shopping at the grocery store, or missing bill payments and having to pay fees, although we had plenty of money in the bank). It came off as unappreciative and frivolous in regards to my efforts for the family.

BEN: My wife doesn't say or do anything that routinely drives me crazy. Seriously.

CHAD: A task needs to get done—say cooking dinner. The end result is the same—dinner gets cooked and prepared properly. I understand the kitchen is her domain, but if I am asked to do something, then isn't it okay I do it my way versus her way—if the end result is the same? Drives me crazy.

My wife gets a thousand questions a day from our kids. The last thing she needs is questions from her husband. However, in order to clarify a task that is getting done by me for her, I may ask an obvious question just to make sure she gets the end result she is looking for. The response I get will be on the sarcastic side because the last thing she needs is her husband asking questions (even though it is in her best interest). Drives me crazy.

JACK: I guess telling me the obvious: "Turn here." "Take out the trash." "We have to leave in ten minutes."

Why do you think it takes a woman longer to warm up to the idea of sex than a man?

BEN: Because, to quote you in the question, sex is *an idea* for a woman. For a man it's a *biological necessity*.

JOHN: Distractions. The average woman—especially a mother—has more on her mind than a man.

CHAD: I hope to find out before I get too old. Actually, I don't think a man has to warm up to the idea, which is probably one of the issues. I think a woman has to somehow purge her brain of all the emotional, kid, house baggage of the day before she is warmed up to the idea of sex. I think feeling loved and meeting emotional needs is a part of the human evolution of the sexual experience for women and not necessarily men.

JACK: Because we are ugly.

11

The Recipe for
a Successful Marriage

LOVING THE ONE YOU LOVE

I'm obsessed with cookbooks. Beautiful cookbooks. Set me loose in Barnes & Noble for even twenty minutes and you will find me directly in front of a table of bestselling cookbooks, eagerly turning the glossy pages. I am attracted to the ones that have fabulous photos of exquisitely coiffed celebrity chefs, slender and smiling over steaming plates piled high with pasta slathered in cream sauce. There is an endless attraction to the food in those beautiful cookbooks, of course, but that is only the beginning of the appeal. Cookbooks are complete—offering a beginning and ending spot. Recipes detail the "how to" with exact measurements for each and every ingredient. No frustrations wondering about getting things right; instead, specific, focused attention on the exact ingredients mixed for success. Why, they even describe how to sprinkle sugar, measure liquids, and tend to batters with utensils appropriate for each and every movement conceivable. And then there are the photos, luminous and opulent, silently declaring the standard.

Marriage is not a cookbook. There are no measurable, perfected recipes for getting through—and that can make for a rather tiring and messy ordeal. Marriage itself is much more like what I experience while bread making. As I am carefully measuring flour, I accidentally knock my elbow against the cabinet, and the flour dumps carelessly on the floor, leaving a spray paint pattern on my bare feet. Minutes later as I yank and pull, relentlessly kneading the sticky dough, I realize I forgot the teaspoon of salt meant to be added with *dry* ingredients. And then finally when all is corrected and nearing summation, I impatiently peek in to check on the dough resting quietly under the kitchen towel and realize the air is too dry to accommodate the rise before dinner. My real-life experience is much more realistic than the glossy cookbook, and I guess that explains my fascination with those cookbooks. I am enthralled with the idea that there is a recipe with a detailed list of specific ingredients and directions for getting just the right result.

Sometimes I long for that kind of simplicity in my marriage. But I know marriage is much more complicated. And there are some days that it is so complicated that even if I had a recipe sitting there in front of me, I would be mystified. But I guess relationships are like that, aren't they? They are messy and unpredictable. And sometimes that can make life ultra-tiring. So tiring, in fact, that it makes things relationally complicated.

Having been married nearly twenty-five years, I've experienced these complications often. I'm going along in a perfect stretch with Will—so perfect in fact that I feel pretty smug about the recipe for success in the marital bliss department when suddenly it happens. I wake up one morning intensely irritated by the man. Or he with me, and we're at odds with each other and all seems a mess.

The curious thing is that many times I'm not even sure how it happened. Did he forget to take out the trash, or did I forget to pick up his shirts at the dry cleaners? Did he miss initiating a date night, or did I rebuff a romantic overture? Did one of us say something completely and utterly thoughtless—and miss the obvious hurt in the other's eyes? Or was it all of the above and more? Maybe you can relate. Without warning, you feel as if you're stuck in this sickening place in the relationship—at arm's length emotionally and physically, wondering if the attraction is gone forever. It's a strange, dark tumble to find your feelings so at odds with the deepest longing of your heart. And it's at those times that marriage just feels like a lot of hard work. So much hard work that you wonder if it's worth the effort to keep trying—and you're tempted to settle into a mediocre marital existence or worse.

Columnist James Collins addressed the issue in an article entitled "Does It Have to Be Work?" and I like where he ended up:

> Much has been learned about the difficulties that can arise between two people who are in love—and how to address them. We now know how to use "I" statements. We know that making a relationship a success involves a huge amount of effort. How many times have you heard a therapist, or a friend, or a friend who thinks he or she is a therapist say that a relationship is hard work? It is a constant refrain—"a relationship is hard work." I have heard this so many times that when anyone says the word *relationship,* I now see an image of sweating slaves in loincloths pulling huge stones up to the side of a pyramid.
>
> Doubtlessly, all these insights are very valuable. But I sometimes wonder whether, while we are toiling away at our long checklist of relational tasks, we have actually forgotten to do something that arguably is as important: actually loving the person we love.
>
> If only it were that easy, you might say. How can we actually love the person we love when we are burdened by resentment and fear and insecurity and anger and narcissism and hostility and self-loathing and bouts of total irrationality—as when, for example, we become furious with the person we love whenever she does something like call us at the office while

155

we are staying late to meet a hugely important deadline to ask again how to work the new DVD player so she can watch *Something's Gotta Give* for the ten-thousandth time?[1]

There is a profound truth buried in the second paragraph. The gem? Collins's assertion that "actually loving the person we love" is vitally important. Yes, I know that sounds incredibly simplistic, yet it's the most difficult "task" I've ever encountered and it's what makes his statement so achingly profound. Because in a lifelong commitment, it's intensely complicated to truly "love the one you love." But I believe it's the key to getting past much of the "resentment and fear and insecurity and anger and narcissism and hostility and self-loathing and bouts of total irrationality" that, if we're honest, we'll confess we all experience in marriage.

Marriages dissolve and grow cold because people stop loving the ones they love. And I'm not talking about the "love" intention—as in "Your father and I will always love each other, but we just can't stay married any longer." I'm talking about "love" in action. The sort of love that stays together—and keeps caring. That keeps trying. That never gives up. The kind of love that in all actuality is the personal achievement of a lifetime. A love that causes you to put aside yourself and put the other person first and foremost—even in the exhaustive, ugly, nitty-gritty of life when all hell is breaking loose and you feel you're at the point of breaking. That's the greatest love of all, and it's how you live out "loving the one you love."

Saying Grace

Tonight we'll attend the wedding of a friend of ours. At the beginning, theirs was a relationship regarded with curiosity and some skepticism by their family and friends. Maybe because they have such different personalities. Or maybe because their family backgrounds were polar opposites.

Honestly, I'm not sure why all the fuss and second guessing. But what I love about the ceremony and eventual union produced by a wedding is that all the musing is a moot point at "I do." At that precise moment when the minister has the couple face the congregants and presents them as husband and wife—'tis a done deal. Commitment begins and the test of "loving the person we love" begins in earnest.

> When two people are under the influence of the most violent, the most insane, most delusive, and most transient of passions, they are required to swear that they will remain in that excited, abnormal, and exhausting condition continuously until death do them part.[2]
>
> George Bernard Shaw

I suppose that's why so many couples, spiritual or not, include portions of 1 Corinthians 13 in their vows. It's as if they understand that they're embarking on a love adventure much bigger than their best intentions or their filmy, lovey feelings. They know it's going to take some serious self-sacrifice to make it "till death do us part." And amongst all the fragrant roses and that exquisite dress, I love that there's a resolute reality there too. Because truly . . .

Love is patient and kind. Love is not jealous or boastful or proud or rude. It does not demand its own way. It is not irritable, and it keeps no record of being wronged. It does not rejoice about injustice but rejoices whenever the truth wins out. Love never gives up, never loses faith, is always hopeful, and endures through every circumstance.[3]

As women, we are wistful for the beauty in life. And just maybe, we're eternally "the bride" in search of the delicate loveliness we see at weddings. But what we often fail to remember is that there is a raw, strong beauty there too. And it is tough and forceful and unyielding. It is the everydayness of "loving the one we love."

157

So how do we achieve that kind of voracity? The kind that marches through the grandest heartache and the most dreadful dreary days of marriage?

We need to realize this: we're breakable. Each and every one of us. And there's not one of us who doesn't need grace—and more grace. Author Anne Lamott says it this way:

> Grace is unearned love—it's the love that goes before, that greets us on the way. It's the help you receive when you have no bright ideas left, when you are empty and desperate and have discovered that your best thinking and most charming charm have failed you. Grace is the light or electricity or juice or breeze that takes you from that isolated place and puts you with others who are as startled and embarrassed and eventually grateful as you are to be there.[4]

It's the gift and beauty of unearned love that sets apart a marriage that works from one that doesn't. Because in the end, there's no perfect marriage . . . only perfected lovers. Lovers who understand grace and mercy. The kind who, in a transcendent way, "say grace" over their whole relationship, their whole life.

Many of life's failures are people who did not realize how close to success they were before they gave up.[5]

Thomas Edison

Many days—more than I care to confess or even imagine—grace is what keeps Will and me together. And though that may sound startling or terribly unromantic, it's the most freeing thing I've ever experienced. To know that I'm loved unconditionally is an earthly taste of the Divine. And for that, I'm implicitly and undeniably grateful.

The Blessing of All

What you probably need to know is that I struggled while writing this book—not because I lacked enthusiasm over the subject; rather, I worried you might erroneously believe me to be something I'm not. Or that my marriage is something that it's not. I was concerned that you might read my anecdotes and conclude that because there's wisdom here in print, it means I always have my priorities lined up just right. Or by reading this book, you might in some way think I have cracked the code where men are concerned—or even that by my advocating that you read the book closely, there exists a promise that you'll have your man completely figured out by the last chapter. And gracious me, what really worried me is that you might mistake my husband for a man who is completely satisfied day and night because I am the ultimate sexpot of a wife. I only wish. . . .

But that's just not the case. I am not the ultimate wife. And as I stated earlier, I do not have a perfect marriage. When there are no perfect people, there is no perfect marriage—there is no glossy standard. But what I do know about being married is that, though it does take a lot of hard work, the result is immensely rewarding.

To be able to live with a man, love a man, and unravel the mystery of a man is one of the biggest blessings of my life.

I pray—from the bottom of my heart—that it will be one of your biggest blessings too.

Conclusion

Upon rereading this book, I find that in conclusion I just don't have much else to offer other than to gift you with a promise from the only One who is able to do things in your marriage that are miraculous and amazing.

My prayer is that you make this promise from God your continual belief for your marriage—that you would believe that no matter where you are today, things can get better and better with the help of God. That you can truly have the marriage of your wildest dreams with the man you pledged your love and life to.

So now, dare to ask and begin to believe that . . .

God can do anything—far more than you could ever imagine or guess or request in your wildest dreams!

Ephesians 3:20 Message

Notes

Chapter 1 Speed Sex

1. Megan K. Scott, "Best Time for Sex: Oh, 3 to 13 Minutes," *Seattle Times*, April 3, 2008, http://seattletimes.nwsource.com/html/health/2004324032_survey03 .html.

2. Megan K. Scott, "Sex Therapists: A Few Minutes Is Best," SFGate, April 3, 2008, http://www.sfgate.com/cgi-bin/article.cgi?f=/n/a/2008/04/02/national/ a125323D45.DTL&hw=sex&sn=001&sc=1000.

3. Linda Dillow and Lorraine Pintus, *Intimate Issues* (Colorado Springs: WaterBrook, 1999), excerpt at http://www.randomhouse.com/catalog/display.pperl? isbn=9780307444943&view=excerpt.

4. "Why Women Settle for Bad Sex," *The Week*, March 2, 2007, 20.

5. Kevin Leman, *Sex Begins in the Kitchen* (Grand Rapids: Revell, 2006), 149.

6. Lorilee Craker, *Date Night in a Minivan: Revving Up Your Marriage after Kids Arrive* (Grand Rapids: Revell, 2008), 164.

7. Caitlin Flanagan, *To Hell with All That: Loving and Loathing Your Inner Housewife* (New York: Back Bay Books, 2006), 42.

8. "Wit and Wisdom," *The Week*, January 23, 2009, 19.

9. Flanagan, *To Hell with All That*, 43.

10. Mick Jagger, quoted in *Forbes*, "Wit and Wisdom," *The Week*, July 4–11, 2008, 21.

Chapter 2 Is Food the New Sex?

1. Mary Eberstadt, "Is Food the New Sex?" Hoover Institution, Stanford University, February–March 2009, http://www.hoover.org/publications/policyre view/38245724.html.

2. Quoted in Lucy Atkins, "Undercover Story of Sexless Marriage," Telegraph.co.uk, September 13, 2008, http://www.telegraph.co.uk/health/3356386/Undercover-story-of-the-sexless-marriage.html.

3. "Not Tonight, Dear," *The Week*, September 8, 2006, 23.

4. Kurt Soller, "Weight Loss: Why Guys Don't Diet the Way Women Do," *Newsweek*, March 5, 2009, http://www.newsweek.com/id/187802?from=rss.

5. Leman, *Sex Begins in the Kitchen*, 149.

6. Anonymous male, quoted in Laura Schlessinger, *The Care and Feeding of Husbands* (New York: HarperCollins, 2004), 126–27.

7. Marabel Morgan, *The Total Woman* (Old Tappan, NJ: Revell, 1973), 111.

8. Gary Langer, "American Sex Survey," October 21, 2004, http://abcnews.go.com/primetime/news/Story?id=156921&page=1.

9. Anonymous male in Schlessinger, *Care and Feeding of Husbands*, 126–27.

Chapter 3 Superman

1. Betty Friedan, *The Feminine Mystique* (New York: Norton, 1977), 18.

2. Betty Friedan quotes, ThinkExist.com, http://thinkexist.com/quotes/betty_friedan/.

3. John Eldredge, *Wild at Heart: Discovering the Secret of a Man's Soul*, http://www.ransomedheart.com/ministry/book-wild-at-heart.aspx.

4. Rick Johnson, *The Man Whisperer: Speaking Your Man's Language to Bring Out His Best* (Grand Rapids: Revell, 2008), 19.

5. John Eldredge, *Wild at Heart: Discovering the Secret of a Man's Soul* (Nashville: Thomas Nelson, 2001), 6–7.

6. Video interview with Steve Harvey, April 16, 2009, http://www.abcnews.go.com/GMA/Books/story?id=7347306&page=1.

7. Elizabeth Gilbert, "Q & A with Harvey Mansfield," *O Magazine*, April 2006, 228.

8. Eldredge, *Wild at Heart*, 35.

Chapter 4 Get Over Your Naked Self

1. Faith Hill, "Posing in a Bikini on Magazine Cover My Birthday Gift to Myself," Fox News, October 20, 2008, http://www.foxnews.com/story/0,2933,441181,00.html.

2. Jessica Weiner, *Do I Look Fat in This?* quoted in "Nuggets," *O Magazine*, March 2006, 64.

3. Kevin Leman, *7 Things He'll Never Tell You: But You Need to Know* (Carol Stream, IL: Tyndale), 119.

4. Tom Chiarella, "How Men Really Feel about Breast Implants," *O Magazine*, July 2003, 122.

5. Schlessinger, *Care and Feeding of Husbands*, 125.

6. Pamela Druckerman, "French Women Don't Get Fat and Do Get Lucky," *Washington Post*, February 10, 2008, B02, http://www.washingtonpost.com/wp-dyn/content/article/2008/02/08/AR2008020801607.html.

7. Ibid.

Notes

Chapter 5 Are You Laughing or Crying?

1. Robert Provine, "The Science of Laughter," *Psychology Today*, November–December 2000, http://www.psychologytoday.com/articles/index.php?term=20001101-000036&page=2.

2. Ibid.

3. Ula Ilnytzky, "No Joke, Some Patients Laugh through Treatment: Laugh Therapy Used by Some Hospitals Lowers Blood Pressure, Experts Say," AP, November 28, 2008, http://www.msnbc.msn.com/id/27955969/.

4. Buck Wolf, "Laughter May Be the Best Medicine," ABC News, May 13, 2005, http://abcnews.go.com/Health/PainManagement/story?id=711632&page=1.

5. Hara Estroff Marano, "The Benefits of Laughter: Why Laughter May Be the Best Way to Warm Up a Relationship," *Psychology Today*, April 29, 2003, http://www.psychologytoday.com/articles/pto-20030429-000001.html.

6. http://www.quotegarden.com/laughter.html.

Chapter 6 Materialism and the Man

1. "The Starbucks Closings: A Nation Mourns," *The Week*, August 8, 2008, 19.

2. "Why Home Is No Longer Where the Heart Is," *The Week*, August 1, 2008, 39.

3. Vikas Bajaj, "Equity Loans as Next Round in Credit Crisis," *New York Times* (March 27, 2008), http://www.nytimes.com/2008/03/27/business/27loan.html?pagewanted=print.

4. Ibid.

5. "Materialism Not a Good Match for Marriage: Study," Reuters, March 5, 2007, http://www.reuters.com/article/gc08/idUSL059663420070305.

6. David Leonhardt, "To Spend or Save: Trick Question," *New York Times* (February 11, 2009), http://www.nytimes.com/2009/02/11/business/economy/11leonhardt.html?_r=1&hp.

7. Will Davis Jr., *Pray Big for Your Marriage: The Power of Praying God's Promises for Your Relationship* (Grand Rapids: Revell, 2008), 151.

8. Anne Frank, *The Diary of Anne Frank*, as quoted in *Real Simple Magazine*, June 2009, 56.

9. Davis, *Pray Big for Your Marriage*, 153–54.

10. Tim Harford, "Why We'd Rather Work Than Loaf," *The Week*, January 30, 2009, 34.

11. "Retail Therapy Is a Bad Idea," *The Week*, February 29, 2008, 19.

Chapter 7 Marriage and Multitasking

1. "The Folly of Multitasking," *The Week*, October 26, 2007, 45.

2. Suzanne Choney, "Cell Phones Permeate Personal Moments," MSNBC, February 2, 2009, http://www.msnbc.msn.com/id/28896384/.

3. Debra Cassens Weiss, "35% of Professionals Would Choose Black-Berry over Spouse," *ABA Journal*, September 17, 2008, http://abajournal.com/news/35_of_professionals_would_choose_blackberry_over_spouse/.

165

4. Ibid.

5. "Good Week for: Coitus Interruptus," *The Week*, August 11, 2006, 3.

6. Valerie Frankel, "More Sex Means Less Stress," MSNBC, December 11, 2008, http://www.msnbc.msn.com/id/28146086/.

7. Polly Leider, "Try Sex as a Stress-Buster: Study Shows Sex Has Calming Effect, Lasting Benefits," CBS News, January 28, 2006, http://www.cbsnews.com/stories/2006/01/27/earlyshow/saturday/main1248949.shtml.

8. Leman, *7 Things He'll Never Tell You*, 106.

9. Leider, "Try Sex as a Stress-Buster."

10. Flanagan, *To Hell with All That*, 42–43.

11. "Better Your Body with Robin McGraw," *The Doctors*, http://www.thedoctorstv.com/main/show_synopsis/188?section=synopsis.

12. Eve Van Cauter, quoted in Rob Stein, "Scientists Finding Out What Losing Sleep Does to a Body," *Washington Post*, October 9, 2005, A01, http://www.washingtonpost.com/wp-dyn/content/article/2005/10/08/AR2005100801405.html.

13. Stephen R. Covey, *Everyday Greatness: Inspiration for a Meaningful Life*, as quoted in *O Magazine*, October 2006, 70.

14. Leman, *Sex Begins in the Kitchen*, 148.

15. Flanagan, *To Hell with All That*, 28.

Chapter 8 Why Saying Thanks Is a Big Deal

1. M. Gary Newman, *The Truth about Cheating: Why Men Stray and What You Can Do to Prevent It* (New York: John Wiley, 2008), 20.

2. Albert Einstein, quoted in "Wit & Wisdom," *The Week*, March 27, 2009, 19.

3. Ephesians 5:33 (AMP).

4. John Maxwell, quoted in ThinkExist.com, http://thinkexist.com/quotes/john_c._maxwell/2.html.

Chapter 9 From Roommate to Playmate

1. *OK Magazine*, April 15, 2009, http://www.okmagazine.com/posts/view/13401/.

2. Flanagan, *To Hell with All That*, 37.

3. Shaunti Feldman, *For Women Only* (Sisters, OR: Multnomah, 2004), 156.

4. Ibid., 161.

5. Bob Berkowitz and Susan Yaeger-Berkowitz, excerpt from *He's Just Not Up for It Anymore*, http://abcnews.go.com/GMA/OnCall/Story?id=4137184&page=3.

6. Tara Siegel Bernard, "The Key to Wedded Bliss? Money Matters," *New York Times* (September 10, 2008), http://www.nytimes.com/2008/09/10/business/businessspecial3/10WED.html?pagewanted=2&_r=2&em.

7. Craker, *Date Night in a Minivan*, 175.

Chapter 10 The Difference between Cats and Dogs

1. Sally Law, "Everyone Agrees: Women Are Hard to Read," MSNBC, February 5, 2009, http://www.msnbc.msn.com/id/29034232/.

2. Kevin Leman, *Turn Up the Heat: A Couple's Guide to Sexual Intimacy* (Grand Rapids: Revell, 2009), 53.

3. Leman, *7 Things He'll Never Tell You*, 5–6.

4. Excerpted and adapted from Rick Johnson, *The Man Whisperer: Speaking Your Man's Language to Bring Out His Best* (Grand Rapids: Revell, 2008), 84–94.

5. Leman, *7 Things He'll Never Tell You*, xvi.

6. Jay Dixit, "You're Driving Me Crazy!" *Psychology Today*, March–April 2009, http://www.psychologytoday.com/articles/index.php?term=pto-20090305-000001.xml&page=2.

7. Leman, *7 Things He'll Never Tell You*, 79.

Chapter 11 The Recipe for a Successful Marriage

1. James Collins, "Does It Have to Be Work?" *O Magazine*, October 2008, http://www.oprah.com/article/omagazine/200810_omag_love/6.

2. George Bernard Shaw, quoted in "Wit & Wisdom," *The Week*, March 20, 2009, 19.

3. 1 Corinthians 13:4–7 (NLT).

4. Anne Lamott, *Traveling Mercies: Some Thoughts on Faith* (New York: Anchor Books, 1999), 139.

5. Thomas Edison, quoted in "Wit & Wisdom," *The Week*, June 9, 2006, 19.

Susie Davis is the author of several books, including *Parenting Your Teen and Loving It: Being the Mom Your Kid Needs*; a radio host; and a popular retreat and conference speaker. She has a passion for helping people love God and develop healthy relationships. With her husband, Will, she cofounded Austin Christian Fellowship in Austin, Texas, where he serves as senior pastor and she often teaches. They have three children.

Visit Susie's website at www.susiedavisministries.com.

Parenting Teenagers Is a Difficult Adventure

Somehow, your sweet child has changed into a baffling bunch of hormones you barely recognize. With humor and honesty, Susie Davis, a seasoned mother of teens, answers your biggest questions.

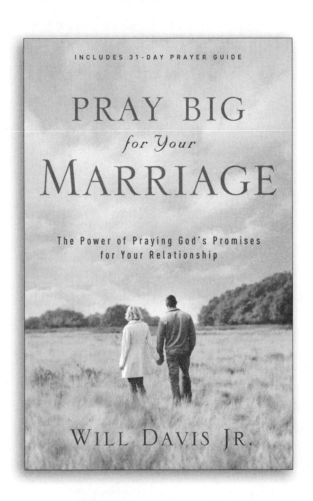

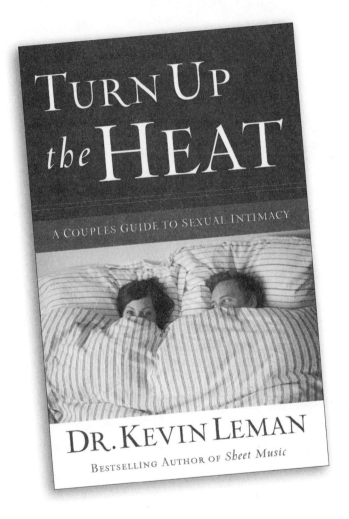